Thomas Irving's Journal

The Memoirs of a Cumbrian Farmer
1851 – 1917

Thomas Irving's Journal
The Memoirs of a Cumbrian Farmer
1851 – 1917

First published October 2008
by
Wagtail Press,
Gairshield,
Whitley Chapel,
Hexham,
Northumberland
NE47 0HS
www.wagtailpress.co.uk

Edited by Hilary Kristensen

© Wagtail Press

Thomas Irving's Journal is reproduced by kind permission from Alex Fotheringham. All rights reserved. No part of this book may be reproduced, reprinted, photocopied or utilized in any form without written permission from the publishers.

Designed by T.W.Kristensen

Printed by Robson Print, Hexham

ISBN: 978-0-9538443-1-9

Contents

Chapter		Page
	Introduction	4
1	Childhood Memories	9
2	Leaving School	13
3	Penrith Hiring 1856	17
4	To Hexham & Bellingham	21
5	Carlisle Hiring at Candlemas	27
6	Thoughts on Ireland	32
7	Buying Sheep & Wheat	37
8	Thoughts on Good Farming	41
9	Starting a New Business	43
10	Marriage & Hazel Cottage Farm	49
11	The Agricultural Holdings Act	53
12	A New Home in Carlisle	59
13	Farming at Newbiggin	65
14	Moving to Lowthian Gill	68
15	1909 & Time to move on	74
16	Micklethwaite & Ghyll Head	83
17	Thoughts on Feeding Sheep	86
18	Good Farming Practices	89
19	Thomas & his Family	93
	Index of names	96

Introduction

Thomas Irving's story was brought to my attention by Alex Fotheringham who had bought the original manuscript, written in pencil, at an auction in Carlisle. The lot also included a framed photograph of Thomas and his wife as well as an edited transcription of the manuscript by his son Timothy J.Irving. Thomas's original punctuation, grammar and spelling, corrected in some cases during the transcription, have been retained.

Fascinated by Thomas's journal, based in and around the Eden Valley, I started to look further into his family history. He gives us some names and dates but frustratingly very few family names. Who were his parents, siblings, wife and children? Eventually through extensive research his relations have been identified and we now have a better insight into his family life.

Whilst Thomas's original story was one continuous manuscript, for ease of reading it has been divided into chapters in this edition. His journal deserves to be shared – it gives a rare, first-hand account of farming and rural life in Victorian and Edwardian Cumbria.

Hilary Kristensen,
Editor

Acknowledgements

Many thanks to Alex Fotheringham, Cynthia Seymour, Fiona Stephenson, Liz Sobell, Gill Smith and Stephen White for their assistance in various ways. Grateful thanks to the following who have kindly given permission to reproduce their archive records and photographs: Beamish Photo Archive – plate 2 (161850) & plate 13 (10152); Carlisle Library – plate 15; Carlisle Records Office – fig.3 (deposit DX132/287) & back cover – section of map of Parton & Micklethwaite Common 1819 (QRE 1/12); Cumbria Image Bank, Cumbria Records Office – plate 4 (ct.5160), plate 7 (ct.5720) & plate 9 (ct.10958). Woodcuts by Thomas Bewick; other illustrations by Pyne.

The first page of the transcription of Thomas's journal made by his son Timothy J. Irving

Farming and Country Life in Cumberland
100 years ago.

Extracts from the Journal, Recollections and Experiences of

THOMAS IRVING

Who, from hired farmer's boy became one of the best-known Yeoman Farmers and Agriculturalists of his time, covering a period of nearly 70 years in the 19th Century.

A keen observer of everyday doings, and a lively and pungent critic on matters of general and family interest, and of the life and times in which he lived.

He practised what he preached, and all his five sons became well-known Yeoman Farmers. The notes were written for the use and interest of his own family, often by the aid of midnight oil after a long day's work.

He died October 18th, 1919, aged 77 years, and was buried at Ainstable, where he was married.

Collected by his son, TIMOTHY J. IRVING, late of Carleton Hill, Carlisle.

the never was in food. the land was of a red nature of soil and what with the wet day and plouding and rolling about the land I was coular to the land and drenched through with with rain. The agent wanted the turnips and stitches split and put in with plenty of moist and he got that to his hearts content. I took my dinner with me from home and when I had finished he gave me 6d for my share. and if I had not been a bad Scholar I would have got well learned to swear what from my master and ploughman to gether, of course I might deserve all I got as I would not be very effecient but I can recollect my poor mother had a improfatable business washing my closes. I met with the ploughman twenty years after and I asked him how the turnips grew he said they were worth nothing we would all have been better in bed. He is a very dour farmer in their days that does not know that seed is better put into the land dry. My next recollection is singling turnips at Blunderpile the same year for 1d per hundred yards there was four of us a sister eleven years old. two school mates a boy of 10 and a sister of twelve. this was for Mr Lewis. we were about through our job and Mr pallister came and engaged us by day we asked him 10d per day and he bid us eight pence but eventually we strucke a bargain at 9d. now it was evident we new our job as. there was the master a man and Servant girl singling with us and we all whent on a stitch each to-gether. The year following we followed the same occupation by the hundred yards and the corn harvest I put in a month at Crindle dyke at ten years of age and a son of Mr Wilson how was twelve shear a rigg betwixt us along with the rest of the hands I was there one month

plate 1 - A page from Thomas's original journal written in pencil

Thomas's Introduction

It has seemed to me a great task to write my life-long experience on agriculture, but if it should be to the benefit of the nation at such a time as Great Britain and Europe are going through at present, I will give my experience and reminiscences of my life of sixty-six years on the land, and the ordeal I have gone through, coupled with what I think and always have thought for the last forty years, how agriculture should be carried on in Great Britain for the benefit of the nation at large.

I have gone through every form of the ordeal, so I do not think any of the great men that are in Parliament, or any of the officials that the Government are giving a big salary to for doing nothing for their money but causing a fallacy, men that are too big for their places and above reason. What I have seen and gone through by experience I am giving free gratis. I think some of my theory that I have written to Editors, but only one published, I suppose thought too broad and before the times, but some of my foresight has been brought into practise, and more of it will have to be before the dear old fatherland is redeemed.

I see I have been before the times, same as Lord Roberts was with wanting the nation to prepare for this dreadful hour that our allies are facing in trying to subdue a country that has been preparing for Great Britain's destruction for more than twenty years.

To explain what I think should be done for the land and bringing the population back to the land, I propose giving my reminiscences back from when I was a boy of nine years of age (1851), up to the present year (1917).

William Irving's Family Tree

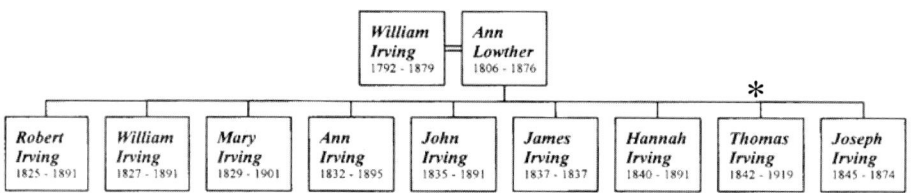

1. WILLIAM[1] IRVING was born 1792, and died 1879. He married ANN LOWTHER 1824.

   Children of WILLIAM IRVING and ANN LOWTHER are:
       i.   ROBERT[2] IRVING, b. 1825; d. 1891; m. RUTH AWDE, 1849.

       More About ROBERT IRVING:
       Emigration: 1856, To Canada with wife Ruth

       ii. WILLIAM IRVING, b. 1827; d. 1891.

       More About WILLIAM IRVING:
       Emigration: 1856, To Canada

       iii. MARY IRVING, b. 1829; d. 1901; m. JOHN LITTLE, 1850.
       iv. ANN IRVING, b. 1832; d. 1895; m. THOMAS LAYCOCK, 1857.
       v. JOHN IRVING, b. 1835; d. 1891; m. ELIZABETH STORROW, 1865.
       vi. JAMES IRVING, b. 1837; d. 1837.
       vii. HANNAH IRVING, b. 1840; d. 1891; m. ROBERT WATSON, 1861.
   *   viii. THOMAS IRVING, b. 1842; d. October 18, 1919; m. MARY ANN RAIN, September 10, 1870.
       ix. JOSEPH IRVING, b. 1845; d. 1874.

1

In 1851 a gentleman Land agent named Isaac Errington engaged me to sow turnips with a drill drawn behind a double plough, splitting stitches. I had to change sides with drill at every land end, not such a pleasant task for a boy of nine, and it was a thorough wet day. We went through Croglin Water to get to the field broad meadows, and when we came through at night the river was in flood. The land was of a red nature of soil, and what with the wet day and ploughing and rolling about the land, I was colour of the land and drenched through with rain. The agent wanted the turnips and stitches split and put in with plenty of moisture, and he got that to his hearts content.

I took my dinner with me from home, and when I had finished he gave me 6d for the share, and if I had not been a bad scholar I would have got well learned to swear, what from my master and ploughman together. Of course I might deserve all I got as I would not be very efficient, but I can recollect my poor mother had an unprofitable business washing my clothes. I met with the ploughman twenty years after, and I asked him how the turnips grew. He said they were worth nothing; we would all have been better in bed. He is a very poor farmer in these days that does not know that seed is better put into the land dry.

My next recollection is singling turnips at Blunderfield the same year for 1d per hundred yards. There were four of us, a sister eleven years old, two schoolmates, a boy of ten and a sister of twelve. This was for Mr. Lewis. We were about through our job, and Mr. Pallister came and engaged us by day. We asked him 10d per day, and he bid us 8d, but eventually we struck a bargain at 9d. Now it was evident we know our job, as there was the master, a man and a servant girl singling with us, and we all went on a stitch each together.

The year following we followed the same occupation by the hundred yards, and the corn harvest I put in a month at Crindledyke at ten years of age, and a son of Mr. Willson who has twelve shear a rigg betwixt us, along with the rest of the hands. I was there one month all but a half day, and my master give 24/-, and I remember I came away as pleased as Punch.

My sister is dead many years ago. She married a man the name of Robert Watson, Manchester Street, Oldham. His mother, he and the rest of her family had a Cloth Dyeing business, and my sister went there to live among them. They all died off, but the youngest sister who got married. My sister took the business on herself after that for a few years, and then her time came to leave this sphere, after a long and arduous life.

The other two schoolmates are both living retired in the house they were born in, at the age of 76 and 78. No old age pensions attached to them, retired upon their own thrift and exertion.

The remainder of the autumn I gathered potatoes and helped on the land, and for the winter quarter I went back to school. The spring came again and I was wanted to help on the land to harrow and help with the seed for Mr. G. Carrick, Westgarth Hill, our nearest neighbour. There until turnip hoeing time and then I went back to that business at 1d per hundred yard. That year I can well mind there was one morning I was going to have a big day. I went off from *home at five o'clock in the morning into a field, belonging to John Thompson, Scales; the field was 200 yards long.*

I singled 14 stitches and addled 2/4d. That was one of the biggest days I ever had at that profession. Moreover, I never saw anyone but myself all that day. Harvest came about again, and I went to help an uncle at Great Salkeld named Peter Smith, with his harvest, only on a small scale. He was an old man, but at all events he and I cut it, led and stacked all our two selves, though great things for age and youth, as they were both two extremes for the job.

I finished up with potatoe picking in the autumn, went back to school for the winter quarter, and in spring I went to help my old neighbour G.C., and followed my old routine of work for him until winter came around, when I went back to school for the winter quarter for my final education.

The school master and my late employer were very great friends, and, however it came about, the school master bought me an Agricultural Class Book, published by Director and the Commissioners of National Education in Ireland 1850. It was the only book of that class that was in the School. Being rather fond of poetry, I took the most interest in what qualities should be looked for in a prime cow given in verse. The following was the text –

She's long in her face, she's fine in her horn,
She'll quickly get fat without cake or corn.
She's clear in her jaws, she's full in her chin,
She's heavy in flank and wide in her loin.
She's broad in her ribs and long in her rump,
A straight and flat back with never a hump.
She's wide in her hips, she's calm in her eyes,
She's light in her neck and small in her tail,
She's wide in her breast and good at the pail.
She's fine in her bone and silky of skin,
She's grazier's without and butcher's within.

I got that off by heart and it is mostly to the point, whatever I missed learning in my present job.

plate 2 - A watercolour painting, dated 1874, of *Siddington 7th* and *Duchess Gwynne*, two shorthorn cows bred by Mr Hetherington of Brampton and owned by the Earl of Bective, Underley Hall.

2

The spring of 1856 came around. I was fourteen years of age in March of that year, and left school for good on April 24th. I had two elder brothers set sail for Canada, North America; they were a good few years my senior, one of them married and the other single. I set them off from Penrith station to bid them the last farewell. There was a big company of them altogether going at the same time. My brother's wife, mother and two brothers, a family of the name of Varty, consisting of father, mother and eleven children. Some more I do not remember. But one thing I do remember, it was a great blow to dear mother to part with those so near and dear. I do not think people take it so badly in these days.

Well, I had done a good bit of work of the kind, and what was useful work for myself and employers, but when one thinks about those times and the craze now in force and some fanatics wanting to compel children to go to school until they are eighteen and make laws that they have not to touch work until they think themselves too good to look at work on a farm, let alone work, and still at the same time crying about bringing people back on to the land. Education no doubt is a good thing, but will it enrich a nation or be any better for the rising generation to follow the course that has been going on for the last fifteen or twenty years, let alone trying to make things worse?

There has been a great outcry about Germany, what she has done for education in the past. She has been teaching thrift as well as education about the working classes, and the upper ten have been teaching militarism, robbery, plunder and barbarism. Education is well in its place, but to make a god of it is wrong, and shun industry in other spheres.

It is an acknowledged fact that from the King and Bishops down to the humblest subjects, a nation cannot exist or have an existence without what the land produces. What have our great statesmen been doing to encourage the productions of the soil this last generation: the question is easily answered; they have done nothing to make laws that have caused the land to be forsaken and the cry has been for a few years – "come back to the land". All the time they have been doing their worst to keep the population off the land, through fads and a mania they have got for education. It is all very well for them that can get an office under the Government and drink the cream of the milk and let the public pay for it, and there are thousands of them that can be done without who have salaries under the Government, and the money could be saved by the state and put to a better purpose. One would have thought some of the land agents would have had a theory to propose to remedy some of the evils and to prevent the deterioration and neglect of the land, but it is not coming their way.

The men that are put into power to make laws will have to mend their ways towards Agriculture and land reform if the land and soil are to be put to the best possible use to the nation at large, and that is what should be done with the land, and that is the purpose that it is there for.

Some of the causes, and the main causes why the land has not been put to the best possible use to the nation are these: the Government making laws to enforce the rising generation not to work, or even look at it until they have attained such an age (fourteen years), and some fanatics are proposing sending children to school until they are eighteen. They certainly are only men that have got education on the brain. Our prosperous farmers of today are men that have brought their families up with teaching them to work as soon as they could toddle about, as well as giving education. Farming and education are instilled into them soon after then can walk. If it had not been for that there would have been no farmers left or not one on the land.

It is a Godsend today; people know it to be so. The Government has driven all the rest of the rising generation off the land, and are making no real true effort to get the population back.

If you want to train a tree to grow, you have got to start with it when a twig. Now to teach children to stay on the land, or if wanting to put them to any other business or profession, start with them when they can bend, and not let them grow until they are too stiff to bend, and more than that, too good to try. Well, poor wee things, they are not to blame, it has been the way they have been taught, the Government compelling them to go to school, and after that their parents no doubt have a warm side for their own dear kin and they think their offspring has got to be a scholar; it would never do to let them doff their clothes to work, so of course they are off to seek some easy job, not to blame.

Well suppose these children were taught to help on the land, say, two months in the summer, at intervals in the busiest season, and the schoolmaster go with them to help the farmer to drill them, or any other business that it would be useful for themselves to do. It would be a holiday for both the children and schoolmaster, and would not be detriment to their education in the least. Children, say from twelve to fourteen years of age, could do a lot of work upon the land to help and improve the same. There will be a dearth on the land if this is not done; it does not want a moment's consideration.

No doubt the women are doing a lot of useful work and the wounded soldiers that are not too disabled to work a bit, but no one can look to them to fill the ranks that have been thinned by the war, and the nation at large should see that all of the disabled who have been tortured in fighting the nation's battle be properly looked after.

I commenced by writing my ups and downs through life, so I will go back to when I left home as a farm servant at the age of 14.

3

I went to Penrith hiring in the year 1856, and engaged to a near neighbour, George Pallister of Blunderfield, for £5.15.0., the summer half year, considered a good wage then for a boy of 14. My friend and late employer was put out of the way that I left and hired, but nevertheless he gave me a better send-off than I perhaps deserved. He told my new employer, when he was enquiring about my abilities, that there were many men not as good. I cannot forget I had a good home, and my dear mother was put out of the way when I left home, although I was going to live so near.

I put the summer half year in there, and we had a fine haytime, but the weather broke and we had a most miserable harvest; just finished leading the Friday before Martinmas Day. The stooks of corn were blown down and got wet and set up again. I know it was sickening, getting wet through so oft with the job. One day in particular we took our vests off and put them under a stook to keep dry, and at noon we were so drenched we took our shirts and put our vest on next to our skins, and walked home with our wet shirts swung over our shoulders.

Well, I stopped on for the winter half-year for the same wage. My master had taken another farm to enter the spring following at Newbiggin Townfoot. He lost his health just before Martinmas and was poorly all winter, and I was the only hand but a servant girl on the farm. I had five horses to look after, twenty-five head of cattle, and a hundred ewes; a stiff job for a lad, until Candlemas when he engaged two more men to go to the new farm, and I was left to look after the ewes on the old farm up to the 25th of March, a right nice job.

The new farmer, Mr. Proctor, came to Blunderfield; he was a Liverpool gentleman farmer, and had served his time to farm with David Hill, a great sheep dealer at that time, and married a niece of Mr. Hill's. Mr. Proctor's parents were well-to-do people, and, or course, they were short of nothing when they came. He brought two beautiful black horses, likewise two dark greys. There was a park called Langmer Park, which was 85 acres. Mr. Proctor's intention was to break it up. It had been laying a long time and grazed with ewes and lambs, but grown very much over with ling, but it grew some wonderful crops of corn.

Well I put my time in up to Whitsuntide at Newbiggin, and then I left and went back to Penrith hiring to try my luck. I drove a bargain with Mr. James Faulder of Great Salkeld at £9 for the half year, hired to be man on the condition I had never stitched or stacked but willing to learn.

I learned to do both jobs through a hind Mr. Faulder had; I cannot say it was owing anyway to my own cleverness. The hind was a thorough husbandman at all branches of husbandry, and only had the small weekly wage of 9/- per week, a free house and a cow kept. They had two children and the mother and himself to feed. They often complained to me that they were very badly off and could not get necessaries. I have seen tears in their eyes when speaking about it; many times I have thought it was no wonder. His wife had been living in gentleman's service before marrying. It would have taken as much to keep herself in the place she was serving in, but at all events they could not get an existence and they spoke about emigrating, and did a short while after.

All went on swimming with me; Mr. Faulder was quite a good master, and a well-living man. I was inexperienced for the place I took in hand.

The summer went on and we had a fine haytime. The horses had nothing much to do, so he arranged to set me off to Talkin Fell coals with two horse and carts. I had to start off at 11 o'clock p.m., one hour before midnight. The distance was about 18 miles. I had to go through Kirkoswald, Craglin, Wath, and past Wallmersyke Mill. There was a sharp turn at that place and sleep had overpowered me, the horses got off the road and went over a dangerous place, a place I would not like to have driven over if I had been awake. Nevertheless, the carts and all kept right side up. I have sometimes thought I would have been in a funny predicament at 1 o'clock in the morning with two horses and carts if anything had happened, but at all events all went on splendid after that, and I landed at Talkin Fell pits about 4 o'clock in the morning, baited the horses there a bit, came back by Castle Carrock, baited the horses there about two hours, and landed back at Great Salkeld about 4 o'clock in the afternoon. The coals were sold by the box there, 1/2d per box. I loaded with four boxes, calculated to be about 16 cwts, 4/8d to the load.
We had an extra fine harvest, and a very good crop of wheat in two fields at the Lum, which Mr. Faulder's son and I led to half way well right of the scythe, never stooked at all, put into a barn for the hind to thrash in winter with a stick and a half, a job that no youth liked, and to set a man at that job now, he would prefer the treadmill.

Well Martinmas came around again, and Mr. Faulder and me could not get a bargain. I wanted my summer wage and he wanted me to take a pound less, £8, likely as much as I was worth, but we parted that way. Harvest was forward and work well advanced, which made hiring dull, I know I had a struggle to get the £8 at the Hiring at Penrith.

I hired for £7.15.0., to go to Mr. Joseph Braithwaite of Ousby, under the East Fell side. I had an older brother lived at the same place, a servant. Also he lived with Mr. Faulder before I entered service with him. My brother was eight years my senior, so I think I would have a difficult job in filling the place as satisfactorily, but the Master and Mrs. were kind to me. They had a son and daughter at home with them, and we all got on together very smoothly.

It was a remarkably fine winter until Easter Sunday. It was in the year 1857-58, and it came on a severe snowstorm on Easter Sunday night. With some more of the youths in the neighbourhood I was drinking mulled ale in the pub at Ousby Hole that night – not a very creditable way to spend Easter Sunday, but when we came out to go home there was about six inches of snow to wade through and in places it was drifting and in the morning all the roads were blocked. All that could be spared got a job clearing the snow from the roads for the traffic. What a change came over the weather. We had it right rough (windy and stormy) through April, but we got seed put into the ground.

4

Whitsuntide came about, and I changed places again. They were all very anxious for me remaining on for the summer, but I think I was more of a rambling disposition, and I preferred leaving, although they were all exceedingly kind to me. I was not of the same disposition as my master. Some the offspring are living there yet, and had done for generations before.

Well I set my face for home on the Saturday and on the Tuesday I went to Penrith to late fresh quarters. I drove a bargain with Mr. John Bird of Eamont Bridge for £11.15.0. for the half year, considered a man's wage at sixteen years old, but taking all into consideration I worked for my stakes. There was just myself and a servant girl. Mr. Bird had a Bacon and Seeds Business in Little Dockray, Penrith, never on the farm but twice during the half year. There was a son and two daughters, and the son was supposed to help me with the work, but he did not incline that way, so the girl and I had most of the work to do outside on the farm. The son and daughters were very kind hearted and good, but I think work was not in their line.

And, as for Mr. Bird, he was thoroughly respected in his trade and was a man that had striven in his younger days and from a farm servant had made himself well to do.
Their dwelling was standing in the right position for getting drink. There was a picture house right in front and another next door. There was a bagatelle kept in that right opposite. The son and I and three or four young men mates often went in the evening to play a game, not without having a drink, and about twice a week we went to Penrith to the theatre or other places of amusement. We were spending

all the fodder on the ground, and I can speak for myself, my wage did not uphold me that half year.

Mr. Bird died shortly after I left. The daughters got married, Frances to Mr. Ibbetson and Ann to Mr. Bradley. The latter did not live long, and her husband was killed on Kempley Brow, falling out of a trap.

In the autumn of the year 1858 there was a great Greyhound Coursing at Broomhall. The dinner has held at Mr. Ibbotson – The Round Table, Eamont Bridge. Mr. Bird, my master, being a neighbour, I was sent off with a cart with drink and provisions to sell and distribute in the fields after the Coursing.
Portland won one of the Coursing, and I backed him from the first day and got three half crowns to one, a simple bet on my part as I could have got a deal greater odds, but at all events he I had the bet with was a welsher, and I just managed to get my own half crown back off him. I got a bit of help and it was shaken out of his pockets.

The corn was cut with the help of what they called Cross Shearers out of Penrith Cross, with hooks and tooth-sickles. These days the work would never get done if it had to be done in the same way, but it has not, thanks to the brains and ingenuity and perseverance of some of our great men.

It would have been well for Great Britain today if agriculture and the improvement of the land, the thing that all, both beast and body, have to depend on for an existence, had made such a stride in the same direction, but instead of that, the buildings, fences, water courses and drains, with which our forefathers did their laborious work is allowed to go to wreck, as it is too much to repair than in those days. Our rulers have driven the population off the land, and they will never return until they stop their fads and stop making officials and giving them £500 to £1,000 a year for doing worse than nothing.

Well, the term came, Martinmas Day, which fell on a Thursday, the 11th of November. I left after dinner, and with a particular chum, John Burns, a neighbouring servant, set off to attend a Goose Feast at Langwathby which was held annually. We sang and danced until well on to breakfast time, and then we walked back to Penrith station, four of us taking the train for Carlisle where we stayed all night with a cook who had the management of the dinner and refreshments at Brougham Coursing (she gave us an invitation when there).

We put Saturday in at Carlisle Hiring, and then we set off for our dear homes. I had about eight miles to walk after taking the train to Southwaite about midnight. When I landed home, had a pair of new wellington boots on, and when I took them and my socks off, the skin came off with them. I could not get about after that for five or six weeks, but it did me good; I had a good home, and it gave me time for reflection.

I put in the winter at home, draining and working days among the neighbouring farmers. When Whitsuntide came near I thought of farm service. Northumberland Hirings were earlier than Cumberland, so I thought I would try Hexham, for a situation. I set off at 2 o'clock in the morning and walked to Brampton station; took the train there for Hexham Hiring, and engaged to a Mr. Thornton of Bewcley. I trained to Brampton again in the evening, walked home 14 miles each way, and landed home exactly at 2 o'clock next morning. I can well remember I was both tired and sleepy.

The Thursday following I set off to my place and landed there. The people were strange to me and their ways a little different, but all went well until end of haytime, and they had what they called a Spa Well Sunday about three or four miles away, and there was a great gathering of young people, and among the rest I thought I would spend the day there, so I did.

I was introduced to a young lady from Bellingham and I accompanied her home. In returning I missed my way and did not land home until the small hours of the morning. All were happy inside and could not hear me, so I got a ladder and got in at my bedroom window. My master took it a great offence and we got unpleasant words about it and I thought it would be best for us to part, so I asked him for my wage as far as I had served, but he refused to give me them, but things were not going on very well and I bothered my master until he have me them on the Wednesday following.

Now I did not want to return home in the middle of the half year, so I set off to seek work on Newcastle Water Works which was going on at the time, but working near a finish. I got a job at one of the shafts at the tunnel, which was about three miles long, winding the rock and refuse out of the tunnel. There were twelve of those shafts down into the tunnel, and I was no longer required. I went further down the tunnel, lifting the rails, etc. for the finishing stroke. The tunnel was about five feet in diameter and it was all rock here and the water was coming out of the rock above; to compare it, it was like a heavy thunder shower.

Now I was not down in the bottom very long until I got a complete drenching; there was a mate working with me who had a tarskin cape on, but I just had an ordinary suit. My mate was very considerate with me, but he could not prevent me from getting wet and a draught in the tunnel, and I got very cold and numb. It was about 300 yards deep here, and only a tub about a foot square to set your feet in and a rope landing at the tip. Just before I got to the top the men who were winding me up gave a loud shout; they likely thought something and they were right, I was just about going off, I did not want any more of this.

During the month I was on this work, on a Saturday pay night there was a row struck up between the Englishmen and Irishmen in a pub. The Irish were the stronger party in the pub, and they struck at nothing that was bad enough. They knocked an Englishman on to the fire grate, and two or three of them were pelting away at him there, and if it had not been for a strong young man who rushed at them and floored a few of them and pulled the man out from among the ruffians, they would have knocked him out.

The next morning (Sunday) the English rose and drove the Irish off the works, and on the Monday morning the rumour got abroad that the Irish had gone across to Bellingham to bring a lot of their own countrymen to do the English in. The Hexham, Bellingham and Ricerton Railway had just commenced construction the spring of that year, and they estimated there were over 500 Irish working there, so the workmen on the water works were called up and formed ranks to meet the Irish, and we marched out about three miles to meet them. We had all sorts of bludgeons and a couple of flutes for the band to play as we marched. We came to an Inn that had a nice green in front and we made a halt and had a supply of drink, ale and spirits. There were two police landed up and they went to meet the Irish and turn them back, so we halted here and had a beautiful picnic – a few barrels of ale were emptied. We got no further and heard no more of the Irish, so we returned home in the evening.

The job in my line on the works was about finished, so I thought I would get a bit of harvesting which had commenced. I fell in about a mile east of Corbridge, binding wheat sheaves behind five Irishmen. I had about a fortnight and as I did not fall in with another job I set off for home. I called at Newbiggin Townfoot to see my old master, Mr. Pallister, and got a job helping him to finish the harvest, and then I set off for home, dear home.

plate 3 - Burnt House, also known as High Westgarth Hill, where Thomas lived with his parents and siblings.

5

I stopped at home until Candlemas, helping my parents with a small Bacon Curing business, draining and working among the neighbouring farmers on odd busy days.

At Candlemas I went to Carlisle Hiring, and engaged myself to a Mr. Benson at Crookdyke Mill, West Cumberland. Stopped there for the quarter until Whitsuntide, and then left for Carlisle Hiring (this was in the year 1860).

My brother, John, and I went and stopped all night with any uncle and aunt on Broadfield. This was on the 29th May, and when we got up on the Sunday morning there were about four inches of snow. After breakfast we went out into the fields; the sun was shining, and it was like the most beautiful Christmas morning that I ever saw.

We set off to see the dear old folks at home in the afternoon, and then for Penrith Hiring on the Tuesday morning, the 31st, and on going over Maidenhill Brow there was a snow wreath just beside Maidenhill Inn at one side of the road. It was a high as the cart naff, the wind having blown the snow through a gate stead. There were a number of sheep blown over on the fells in that storm.

I hired to serve Mr. Abbot of Thornthwaite Hall for the summer half year; it was the third place at which I served where I followed my brother. I was hired as headman, young to have taken such a post, but I was likely possessed of plenty of confidence.

They estimated that there were 200 acres of hay to mow when the time came, and it was just one fine week, the week we commenced.

There were two men who were paid so much to mow by the acre. I was sent to Clifton with a horse and cart to bring them. They brought two barrels of ale or old hock with them, together with their scythes and tackle, and their names were Harry Carrick and John Irving. They liked a glass, and we had to call at every public house we came to, and we all had more drink than was good for us. They boarded with Josse Green, a shepherd at Nadell Forrest, a bit past Thornthwaite Hall, and when we were getting near their lodge, my head not being very clear, going on a brow side I went over a stone with the low side wheel, and when the wheel hit off the stone the cart went right over, broke a cart shaft off and the two barrels of ale went rolling down the hill until a fence stopped them. Luckily both the men were walking and I was riding on the front of the cart, but how I managed to jump clear at the high side I never could tell, but at all events, none of us, nor the horse, was any worse, just the cart.

My master was having his summer holiday at Silloth. I took the cart to the joiner and had it repaired, and when Mr. Abbot came home he heard the news and says to me "What, you got drunk and throw the cart over?" I says "Yes", him in the affirmative. He said "Very well". That was all that was said. Mr. Abbot was a forgiving soul, or I thought at the time I might have had to look for my chips.

The men I brought cut 96 acres, and for the rest of the mowing and hay making there were eight of us part of the time. We were supposed to mow until 10 o'clock, and then work the hay the remainder of the day. I can remember the names of five of them – Joseph Green, George Greenhow (shepherds), Tommy Rose from Eumont Bridge, Tommy Henson, Foxcroft from Shap.

It was a most miserable haytime for rain; many a day we could not look out, lot alone work hay. We just finished hay the Saturday before Broughill Fair. I set off with some two-years-old young horses on the Sunday to Broughill Fair, among them, and we stood two days and all my master was able to sell was the filly at £13. She would have been worth £60 today (thirty years ago).

It was a miserable time for the farmers, the spring being so bad and thousands of sheep were lost, owing to the snow and bad weather; it was a heartbreaking time for the farmer. The weather did not improve; we only had a few acres of corn and it was hard to get in.

In the autumn they that could soap sheep commenced work on them. Their wool had to be shaded a little distance apart with the fingers and thumb, about three inches apart, and the soap put on to the skin with the two forefingers. The soap was composed of tar and firkins of strong butter, unfit for family consumption. I had to get the harvest finished and the potatoes out of the ground. I was only a novice among the sheep, husbandry being more in my line.

Martinmas term came and I left for home. I can well remember going through Bampton, a village about a mile away from Thornthwaite Hall, and standing and looking at a field of hay for a few minutes. Half of the field was not cut and the other part was standing in cock, a grand crop. I thought it was no credit to the gentleman it belonged to, but there it was. There are always odd people who make not attempt to get things done in order, and this no doubt, was such an instance.

I stood Penrith Hiring on the Martinmas Tuesday and was hired to Mr. Thomas Fiddler of Plumpton, this being the fourth place of service where I followed my brother. He lived at Thornthwaite Hall previous to my going, and they spoke well of him there, whatever I was considered to be.

I entered on here; there were two draughts of horses. The other servant was James Johnston, a native of Plumpton, and we were hired to do the same work, the master being the head man. We drew for the draughts of horses and ploughs, and we got on very well, put in a comfortable winter and were masters of our work.

In the spring there were one or two incidents I do not forget. My master and I were in a field by the roadside, and two gentlemen happened to be going past, riding on horseback. I asked him who they were, and he said they belonged to the land agent fraternity, adding that farming would never be a very pleasant job until there was a shooting day of that sort of fellow. I thought at the time it was a cruel remark to make, but Mr. Fiddler, being a highly respected gentleman, must have had some grievous harm done to him, but nothing more was said.

It happened some little time after there were a few young men in the Bulls Head Inn, and I was there among them. Not a very creditable place in which to spend one's evenings, but at all events, it happened to be so, and in the meantime two gentlemen came in, one of them being the land agent fraternity, and the other a neighbouring farmer.

They each had a stick, and without any provocation they began to strike us young men on the head with their sticks (they would each be about twenty stones) as if they were felling rats. Never in all my experience had I met with such brutes.

There was a little chap with us, weighing about ten stones, who professed to a bit of wrestling, and butted one of the brute beasts and laid him out on the floor, and after that the two men went away very quietly. Nothing serious happened; two or three had lumps on their heads due to the knocks from the sticks, but I thought there were some grounds for Mr. Fiddler's remarks.

6

There was a time in Ireland (about thirty to forty years ago), when no doubt the people were oppressed by that class of man, and the tenants were so bitter that some of the bloodsuckers were shot, and now the Irish have more liberty than the rest of Great Britain.

It is a great pity that the whole of Ireland does not fall in to a man with the rest of Great Britain and her Colonies and help to crush Germany and her confederates, and to stop for all time the wicked course she is taking. If they should only think for a moment of the destruction and misery she is causing in overrunning her smaller, neighbouring nations, laying them in waste, ruin and misery, all the work of the Kaiser and a few of his subject in high command, and they pray to God that they may be allowed to do more destruction. Is it possible that God will answer the Kaiser's prayers? It is a wonder a man like the Kaiser dare mention the Lord our God at all, but it is the devil who has got hold of him and caused him to display this brutality.

Why doesn't Ireland, and the rest of the world stop in and stop war in all its forms. Look at the misery it has caused, and is causing, to every nation implicated in the war. Think of the brave men who have had limbs flown off and been maimed, and the misery it will cause hereafter, and all of it due to the Kaiser and a few of his leading followers for greed and ambition, for they are aiming at more territory.

What benefit will any of Germany's allies get after the war? The Kaiser and his confederates will treat them as dust. Cannot Ireland see to a man what would come to her if she were to be governed by a nation like Germany? Ireland

and the remainder of Britain can get on well together. At the present time they are getting a living by one another, so why cannot the whole of the British races sail in one boat at a time like this and crush militarism out of existence.

There is no doubt that Lloyd George is a clever man and has done all that a clever statesman could do in carrying the war through to victory, but he and the Government has made mistakes; they have had no foresight when passing measures to revalue the land, and stocked the country with Government officials; two million a year going to land, and stocked the country with the very men that Ireland is dispelling out of Ireland. In these times a more profitable job might be found for the very class of men which is doing harm to their own profession; the money might have been spent in erecting dwelling-houses and making other improvements on the land, and the officials given a hack and spade to work with, instead of a motor-car, lavishing public money about. This sort of work will have to stop, and the sooner it is, the better it will be for the British nation.

Whitsuntide came, and my brother had come in the spring to sow the corn and help in with the crops. My brother and I hired for the summer half year with Mr. Fiddler, and James Johnston hired to a brother of Mr. Fiddler's who farmed High Wool Oaks.

My brother and I spent the summer together; we were true mates as well as brothers. Martinmas came around, and I went home to help our parents with their little business, and worked among the farmers, in spare time, but my brother stayed on, leaving at Whitsuntide. Neither of us hired for the summer half-year, and were at a loose end as it is called, perhaps rightly named.

Haytime came around and we set off to Kirkby Stephen for haytime places, and hired to a Mr. Fothergill. He was not ready for haytime for about a fortnight, so we took the train to Barnard Castle, stayed all night with a particular friend and customer of father's, a carrier and dealer between Penrith and Barnard Castle. Some time previous to this he had travelled with his carts to Dumfries, a fair stretch for horses and carts, but such had to be done in those days.

In the morning we left to go over the hills and dales to Fosterly in Weardale, took some mowing next morning and started cutting grass right away. It was the right kind of weather for haytime, and we were offered more work than we could do. After we had worked about a week my brother strained his side, and when the time came for us to go to our new work he was not fit to go, and as there was more work than I could do in the time, we sent Mr. Fothergill a letter saying we could not go, giving the reason; the unforeseen had happened, and we had to disappoint one or the other.

We stayed at an inn at the east end of Fosterly for a month, and we only had one wet half day and that was when we were leaving. We started off to walk home by Alston, each carrying scythe and bundle, and it was both windy and raining. We set off at six o'clock and landed at Alston about noon, where we had refreshment and stayed a while to dry our clothes, and then set off again for home, near Kirkoswald. The distance was about 36 miles, and I know I was tired. The next day was Sunday, and we were so tired we could scarcely get up for dinner.

My brother John died at the age of 57 at Plumpton, and James Johnston farmed Durdar House Farm, which spoke well of his perseverance in life. He has gone to his rest too.

I hired to Mr. Simpson of Roman Way, Plumpton, for a month's harvest, put in the winter draining and jobbery, and helping neighbouring farmers as well as assisting my parents in the business.

The summer came, and at haytime a friend of mine, William James of Springfield, Kirkoswald, and I went to Kirkby Stephen Hay Harvest Hiring. He was hired to go to a place on the Ingleton railwayside, and I hired to go to a Mr. Thompson, Garsdale Hall, for a week, and then for a month to Mr. John Hanley of Garsdale. This was in the summer of 1863. I put in a month's harvesting with Mr. Fiddler, my old master and friend, and then went home and worked for about a week for Mr. Threlkeld, Highbank Hill. This was my last shearing; it was nearly finished with, but Mr. Threlkeld was an old man and hard to convince that harvest could be done without shearing it, and grubbing all the day long with your nose to the ground. Mowing has superseded it with a scythe and heck.

I spent the winter with my parents and followed the jobs I had done the previous winter. In the spring I took a fresh job in hand, helping Messrs. Watson to erect a dwelling in Kirkoswald back street, and then to build one for Mr. Hodgson at Little Salkeld.

Haytime came around, and I had promised Mr. Hanley to go back and help him with his hay harvest. He wrote to me and we made a bargain, and I set off for Garsdale on the borders of Yorkshire. It was lucky for me as far as finance goes.

I bought what bacon Mr. R. Watson had, a mason for whom I was working in the building line. He cured a few pigs in the winter. I bought it to be weighed there and then, but it had to be hung back until the autumn, when I had to lift and pay for it. The bacon went up and it left me about £12.

7

Mr. Hanley, for whom I was hay-making, had a part where he summered about 100 ewes. I made a deal with him and bought his lambs, about 100, to be lifted about the middle of August at 18/- each, and I bought 40 more from a neighbour, Mr Hutchinson. My brother John was a partner in this transaction, as it took both of us to raise the money.

When the time came for lifting I set off by train to Sedbergh, thence by foot to Garsdale, gathered the sheep up and settled for them. Set off next morning to drive them to Plumpton; got to Tebay the first day, a good stride of about 17 miles. Next day to Shap, about 8 miles, stopped all night at the Greyhound; the sheep were very tired before I reached there. I had an early start the next morning – 4 o'clock, so that I could land them at Plumpton by evening. They were growing very tired, and I had many a good look at them, wondering if they were cheap or dear. I know about as much of the value of them as the dog I had driving them, but I was guided in the buying of them by the price they made the previous year. I had different valuers on the road when driving them, varying about 6/- a head in the valuation.

I got them to Plumpton just as Mr. Fiddler and his men were coming out of the harvest field. I put them in one of his fields, and he bought them off me at 21/6d each, and I was engaged for a month's harvesting, commencing next morning.

I worked my month, and went to a sale of wheat at Ainstable. It was uncut and green and belonged to a Mr. Graham who was obliged to quit his holding on account of

plate 4 - Ainstable village c.1900. The Crown Inn is to be seen in the centre whilst the village shop is on the right.

him being short of finance, not on account of him being a bad farmer as he was up-to-date in that business. It was a grand crop but a risky speculation as it was late for ripening, but the weather was good and crowned it. It was left to women to shear by stook.

My brother, James Birkett and I joined and bought the lot, about 14 acres. We housed and thrashed it with sticks in a barn at Ainstable Towngate. It gave somewhere about 17 Carlisle bushels per acre, and made double what we gave for it, our labour thrown in. This was in 1864.

I spent the winter at home with my parents, helping them and working at draining and farmwork in my spare time. I also worked on road repairing in Staffield high quarter for a Mr. Bell who was appointed Road Surveyor for that district. A brother-in-law did most of the work, and I took it on his account, it being the first time it was let. My father's landlord, a Mr. Ellwood, was an overseer.

Whitsuntide was approaching, and I had been helping Mr. Proctor of Blunderfield on the farm, and he wished to hire me for the summer half year and I engaged to him. I can remember the best of harvests when I was there, and an eighty-five acre park Mr. Proctor broke up the year he entered the farm; this would be eight or nine years after I was hired to him.

It was an unusually heavy crop of oats; one George Davidson and I mowed it with scythe, and I know we had the sweat taken out of us when we were at it. I was living on the place when Mr. Proctor entered with Mr. Pallister, and well I can remember carting a few turnips up on to the park in winter to about eighty black-faced ewes. The park was all grown over with ling and whins then, and I took the turnips to keep them alive; it was a very rough winter for snow and storm. `

I thought at the time when I was harvesting there was a great change; this sort of change is what our great statesmen and rulers should have been making the last forty years. Anyone could have seen, if they had given it a thought at all, that everything gets its existence from the land, which should have been put to the best possible use for the needs of the nation, but lo, where are we at this moment? The war certainly has brought calamity with a crash, but it would have come if there had been no war.

8

Fifty to sixty years ago Scotland was sending her produce, beef and mutton to London and the provincial market, but now Scotland is consuming it herself. The foreign countries who have been supplying us with our needs would stop through time there is not doubt, but what if the worst did not happen. Why should we have forsaken our land at home to send our capital out of the country, and stock the country with paid officials who are doing no good to anybody but themselves, and at a time when the nations is burdened with expense the Government is still heaping the fire higher and higher with unnecessary expenditure. They could find a lot of the officials a more needful and profitable job, and if they could not, let them find one for themselves.

There are men appointed in the different parishes, district councillors or men of rather more than ordinary importance, whom I am told get nothing, it is an honour having the job, and along with them there are a couple of land agents at a high salary, and an office and a clerk or two to keep for no good. They come around saying what has to be ploughed to raise corn to provide the population with food, which is very important and no doubt urgently needed. Is there a single land agent who has thought or made a study of the kind of land that should be ploughed out to make the extra supply of cereal for the community and to give the best results from a national point of view? The men with the big salaries give the orders that each farmer has to plough so much, according to the Committee's views, or their own, never viewing the different farms to see whether it would be prudent to plough so and so, or whether it would be better to plough this land out and let the other land lie.

There are farmers who have grazed certain land, caked their stock on it and manured it, and done everything conceivable to improve this land, and such land is more valuable the way it is lying then ploughing it out and getting a middling crop on it, or a crop that will lodge and be worth very little. I know it would be dangerous for any ordinary person to dictate to those gentlemen who have swallowed the map and in authority.

Now there are thousands of acres of land lying waste, or grazing a ewe or two per acre, or summering a few cattle that are just getting an existence. Such land has been ploughed at some time and known to produce good crops of corn, and would do it again if it was ploughed up and give better results than ploughing the best of the grassland out that is worth ten times as much as the other is for grass, simply that it has been prepared on the surface for that. The other pasture land has been lying waste and it would be fresh and grow if turned up for three or four years, and then it would want managing, and it is coming to that, that it will have to be managed.

I am speaking from sixty five years' experience on the land, and what my father and a neighbouring farmer taught me, and they would have been about one hundred and thirty years old if living. My father was trained in the military at Appleby when peace was proclaimed in Bonepart's time of war over one hundred years ago.
They used to say, give the land something to eat and it would work; land was like a man, if he got nothing to eat he could not work.

9

The term came and I left Mr. Proctor to go home for the winter again, and this was Mr. Proctor's last year at Blunderfield. Candlemas came and I went over the help at the sale. They left, and what came of them after that I cannot say.

The road repairing I was doing at Staffield High Quarter was finished satisfactorily. This was settled by the Surveyor and Overseers; I cannot see why a surveyor was needed at all as the farmers were in turns every year to supervise the roads and do the parish work, but now a District Councillor has to have a horse and trap yoked up to go to Penrith, 12 or 14 miles once a fortnight to report a gutter that needs cleaning, or any other trivial matter. There is an office to be rented in Penrith, and the Councillors from the different areas go to meet there, and there are perhaps one or two with more conceit than the rest make a speech, and it is seconded and a Committee appointed to go and look at a two-penny-half-penny job, with, or course, a motor car hired, a very nice outing if a wet day!

If all this expense went towards repairing the roads they would be a good deal better than they are, and more, this is another instance of impoverishing the rural Districts and taking the money into the towns, whereas the work could be executed in a schoolroom at home in a parish among the rate payers.

It was drawing near to Whitsuntide, and Mr. Isaac Dodd of the Dale came to hire me to work for him, which I did for the summer half year, and this was my last of farm service.

I took a fresh view of things, and thought I would do a bit at the butchering business; I knew nothing about it but thought I would try and learn. My master, Mr. Dodd, went with me to a neighbour, Messrs. Bowman, to judge and help me to buy a few sheep for a start. We made a deal and I had six weeks in which to lift them. I went out among the neighbours for orders for mutton, and then delivered it in a basket. This went on through the winter, and I helped my parents with their business as well.

My brother went down to Carlisle Sands and bought 100 lambs to winter among the farmers, in which deal I was a partner. We sold them at April Fair and they lost £24, a very bad deal, the times being against the speculation.

I thought I would have a horse, and went to look at one that Mr. Joseph Holliday of Low Grounds had for sale. When I got there he hud two young two-year-olds ploughing, and would sell me either. He had brought them right out of the fields, put the gear on to them and yoked them straight into plough. However, I bought the lesser priced one at £16 and a crown, a pretty colt. I took it home, and a younger brother and I yoked it into a cart, very quiet. Father had about 5 cwts of bacon to go to Alston, a distance of about 14 miles. We yoked it up on a Saturday morning, fine and moonlight, and set off with it. It went very quietly and nicely until we drew near Hartside top, and then it turned too quiet and was to drive and before we got to Alston it was nearly tired out.

We finished our business and started for home with the empty cart, but before we got very far the horse wanted to stop every 20 yards or so, and instead of landing home about 6 o'clock, it was 11 o'clock, the horse fairly worn out. It took a bit to bring it round, but with kind treatment it was all right and I sold it at Candlemas for £22.

I thought I would buy one more seasoned, and bought one late in the spring in Sandgate, Penrith, and it turned out all right.

College Park grass letting came on, and I went to take a field. I took what they call "cross acres", 5 1/2 acres joining Berrimoor High Bank Hill, at £25.10.0. To the best of my recollection I bought three or four ewes and three cattle and stocked it. I know it did not make much profit, but I was getting experience.

I had my new horse by now, and I bought a butcher's cart from Mrs. Mason of Walmersyke, so I was fit up for the butchering trade. I had not the customers to keep me regularly employed in that business, so I bought other things, such as pigs, corn, eggs and fruit, and took it to Alston Moor, along with part bacon belonging to the old folks at home. I used to start about 2 o'clock in the morning for that journey, it took about 5 1/2 hours to do the journey. It was a hardy life, but that I have always had, and cannot say I am any better or worse of it today. That is fifty-one years ago, in 1866.

I took a little field off my father's landlord in which to graze my horse, and when August came I bought a few fat sheep off him. He was a great friend to me, and said I could pay for them when it suited me, so I extended my butcher's business.

I bought two fat cattle off William James of Springfield; killed one every alternate week. By now I had got that I

plate 5 - Portrait of Thomas and Mary Anne taken at the doorway of Lowthian Gill farmhouse, c.1900, by Fred W.Tassell of Carlisle. They were married on 10th September 1870.

could kill and dress a sheep myself, but a fat beast was more than I dare tackle, but I had a friend, John Goulding, who came and helped me. He had been in the trade before, so was not long in teaching me how to do that as well.

It was a very out of the way place, Burnt House, standing by itself in the middle of a field with no other dwelling near, so all had to be taken in the cart.

I extended my round as far as seven miles from home. One round I had was to Low House, below Armathwaite, and to the parson, Mr. Kemble, near Southwaite. I worked up a nice country trade; it took time as there were other butchers travelling who had been on before me.

I started killing some nice light cross hogs I bought off Mr. Ellwood, and they were very much in favour with three or four of my best customers.

A Mrs. Ramsey, Low House, Armathwaite, had a winter residence in Edinburgh, and I used to send them a whole sheep carcase there once a week. Also, a Mr. Little, a lawyer, had Armathwaite Castle for a while. He came from Oldham in Lancashire, and when he left I used to send a carcase to Oldham now and again. Light mutton is all the run now, but during the time of which I am speaking it was the exception. This was in the year 1867.

I kept on at the business for the next three years, and in 1870, September 10th, I took myself a partner for life, and I got the cage before I took the bird.

Thomas Irving's Family Tree

1. THOMAS² IRVING *(WILLIAM¹)* was born 1842, and died October 18, 1919. He married MARY ANN RAIN September 10, 1870.

Children of THOMAS IRVING and MARY RAIN are:
    i. WILLIAM³ IRVING, b. 1871; d. 1872.
    ii. GRACE RAIN IRVING, b. 1872; d. 1881.
    iii. WILLIAM LOWTHER IRVING, b. 1873; m. MARY ELIZABETH BLENKINSOP, 1898.
    iv. TIMOTHY JOSEPH IRVING, b. 1874; m. JANE WALTON, 1900.
    v. ANNIE JANE IRVING, b. 1875; m. JOSEPH FAWCETT, 1908.
    vi. JOHN SALKELD IRVING, b. 1877; d. 1952; m. EUNICE LILLIAN FAULKNER, 1907.
    vii. HANNAH MARY IRVING, b. 1879.
    viii. THOMAS JAMES IRVING, b. 1880; m. GRACE GLENDINNING, 1900.
    ix. ROBERT RAIN IRVING, b. 1882; m. MARY PICKERING, 1918.

10

The Midland, Carlisle and Settle Railway was just being made in the spring of that year, and having my principal trade at Armathwaite and neighbourhood, I took two rooms off Mr. John Reay at the south-end of the village, together with a potatoe house which opened out on to the street. I fitted it up for a shop and other conveniences for slaughtering in and a stable for the horse. I was there for 17 months and did a nice trade.

In the summer of 1871, Hazel Cottage Farm came into the market for letting, a farm of 60 acres belonging to the Earl of Lonsdale, about a mile from where I was living. I offered £70 per annum and was accepted as a tenant, to enter at Candlemas 1972. I gathered implements and chattels to prepare for the farming line – I was set on being a farmer. With my other business in the neighbourhood it was just the very place for me. The farm had been tenanted by a farmer who had got into law circumstances and the land and place had gone to rack and ruin. There was only one cartload of dung on the place when I entered, and it belonged to a carter who was living on the place, and he led it away. There were two haystacks standing which made £5 and £7.15.0., and four corn-stacks which made £3.10.0., to £5 each, although you could scarcely call them corn-stacks – brackens, corn and weeds and filth mixed.

My brother was agent for Landales Manure at the time, and I had the motto that my father and tutor had impressed on me, and it was evident that the land wanted something to eat so that it could work, so I ordered some of the best Landales Manure, this being a good firm at that time.

I did not put it on sparingly and I built a small manure works to make my own, and with this and the slaughterhouse dung, it told a tale in the right direction.

Mr. Thomlinson came to Armathwaite Castle at the same time, and he took Armathwaite Mill and land as well, which had been farmed by the same farmer as Hazel Cottage, and the land was in a worse, poverty-stricken, wasted plight than the farm I took, if it could be any worse. Mr. Thomlinson offered to let the land to me, with the exception of a meadow which he wanted to keep, and he being a customer I bid him £20 per annum, but he did not accept my offer. He let it to a Mr. Tweddle of Barnwood, who had it for two years and did nothing at it, so it was going from bad to worse.

Mr. Tweddle gave it up as it was of no value in that state, and Mr. Thomlinson asked me to make a bid for it again. I wasn't very keen but told him I would give what I had bid for it, £20. He likely tried someone else as he was a long time considering the matter, but on the 23rd April he sent the coachman to say I had to have the land. I thought it would have been a deal better if he had let me know sooner as there were 10 1/2 acres lying in oat stubble, and had been for three years, grown over with thistles and other rubbish, and was no use to anybody as it was, and as it was heavy, stiff clay land, it was too hard and too late on in the year to do anything with it for a crop, but I said I would take it. So in June I set to work and cut a crop of thistles and rubbish off it, which I burned, and a soon as I could in the autumn I ploughed it, and we sowed turnips on it.

No one could recollect ever seeing any turnips on the land before. 4 Acres joining the highway, the best of the land, *was grown over with whins, briers and other rubbish; we cleared it off, burned and cropped it.*

I had been doing all I knew to improve the land at Hazel Cottage, at the same time turnip it out of lea without taking a white crop off it, but to my annoyance I had two fields which joined the Armathwaite and Aiketgate road for a distance of 400 to 500 yards, with three gateways in different places leading on to the main road. A large plantation lay on top of a hill, which they sold. There was no access to the plantation except by going through these two fields, and the wood was cut down, trailed on to these fields, carted across to the different gateways, and for something like eighteen months the buyer of the wood took the use of those fields a deal more than the farmer; the fields were about 23 acres, more than a third of the farm. They gave me no recompense for the use of the fields, the gatepost was broken off and gates broken to pieces, and I had to threaten them with a solicitor's letter before I got them to repair the damage. Of course the agreement when letting specified that the landlord could lead timber off the land without paying damage, but any reasonable beggar would have had some compassion under the circumstances.

Well, I continued to make the best of things and do my duty to the place, and all went on smoothly until there was a whinstone cut through by the Railway makers joining my land on the other side of the farmstead and joining the main road to Armathwaite. A gentleman in that trade came to see it, and he decided to take it and open a quarry out in this particular field. He put a siding on the railway and commenced business, butting this 10 acre field right through and across the middle of the field, and a branch of the rail track up into another field to put a stone breaker in, which laid this and another field into one as far as the hedges were concerned. It was making things look gloomy from a farmer's point of view, but nevertheless it was employing labour and so doing good in that direction.

plate 6 - Armathwaite Mill c.1890

11

Well, the Agricultural Holdings Act came into operation, the first of the kind and the best as far as my experience teaches me, simply because it did the least harm of any that have been made since. The House of Commons has been modelling and remodelling Land Acts at times ever since, and I would like to know, and would be pleased to hear if it was correct, if they had done any good. They made one claim, they gave the farmer leave to sell the crop he grew on the farm, but that was only to keep the rents up. It suited the land agents if they could draw any more rent out of the farms they had to deal with, the land they were robbing was of no consideration to them. They never made any endeavour to keep the rural population on the land; they made agreements between landlord and tenant, and caused no end of confusion and irritation between the off-going and on-going tenant, then the agent was called in to decide and they lined their pockets ten guineas a day, the agents drawing up conditions and the Government breaking them with measures they passed, and the agreement of let treated as the Germans treated the Treaty they had made with the Allies, as a scrap of paper. The agents are allowed to do things that no moral or lawful person would do. These are facts and they are put in for that purpose.

Well, the Agricultural Holdings Act came into force, and the Earl of Lonsdale's tenants could either have their farm as conditions specified, or under the Act, but the farms had to be revalued and a different valuation put on to it if the tenant preferred to have it under the new Act of Parliament. So the land agents were sent around to value the different estates of the Earl of Lonsdale.

Mr. Richardson of Carlisle was appointed to value the Armathwaite Castle Estates and a Mr. John Hope of Rock Lodge came around with him. They came to go over mine one very fine morning and went leisurely over it. He first came over one field and passed a remark on the good management it showed; he went through all the fields and several times spoke of the good order and condition. I asked him if he knew the place before, and he said he had known it all his life and it was as poor a place as ever a crow flew over, and Mr. Hope said that Mr. Richardson was utterly surprised at the state of management I had it in, and he said I would make my mark some day. "Well", I thought, "I must be getting to be a farmer now".

Well, things did not go on as rosy as this for very long. We had brought up a young hound the year before at the then Earl of Lonsdale's wish, or his agent's, along with the rest of their farmers; got praise for making them grow into such fine dogs. The one we had had given us a bit of annoyance among the children, and by stealing into the slaughterhouse and helping itself to a carcase of mutton two or three times, so my wife said we would have no more of them.

However, the officials – four of them – landed down at the door with a coach and pair and another lot of pups to distribute as before. I happened not to be at home, but my wife was there. They sent a boy in off the road to leave us one of them, but my wife told him we did not want one, so with a little to do he took it back to the conveyance, but the boy and the trainer landed back into the house with it, but the Mrs was not to be done; she told them we did not want it, so they went back to the coach with it. But they weren't going to be shaken off. Mr. Mounsey, the steward, insistent about it, but my wife said she would rather not have it and would rather pay for someone to bring it up than have it. He said it would not do to go back to the Earl of Lonsdale with it, but she still said we would not have it, so that was a finish to it.

The others they left in the neighbourhood and would get a pile off some of them; at all events they would get none of them back to Lowther. I cannot think that they were ever sent by the Earl, but by all events no more pups ever came to Armathwaite district to be brought up.

At all events it caused a storm to brew at Lowther, and it landed down to our place with a hurricane. I received a letter from Mr. Mounsey that I had to cut all the thistles in the field where the quarry was, as there were as many as would sow all Hesket parish with seed, and moreover I had to dress the roadside of whins, briers and rubbish, a part that did not belong to me. A stone wall was my boundary fence and this rubbish had been there for a generation.

Well, I began to think of what Mr. Richardson had said previously praising the management of my farm, and thought this I was wanted to do was hardly the thing, so I took the letter I had received and showed it to Mr. Richardson, but all the consolation I got was that I had better go home and eat humble pie. Mr. Mounsey likely thought he would make the hound bite us hard at any rate.

In a very short time after I got a notice from Mr. Thomlinson that I had to quit the mill land which I had taken off him. This also belonged to the Earl, but Mr. Thomlinson had relet it to me. Well the field in which they had been making the excavation for a train line was cut into four different pieces and made absolutely useless to me at the time. I had paid my rent two or three times without any reduction, so I applied for an allowance, but they were very slow in coming forward to make me any recompense. I approached them three or four times, and eventually a land agent, the gentleman who had the management of the quarry, and the Earl's steward came down to value the damage I had suffered. They drove up to the door in a coach and pair and told me their errand, so we went over it. I got the award two or three months later, my share for the damage done being six guineas, and the agent's fee was three guineas. I calculated it to be about 1_d per time for putting the stock right, not to speak about the loss I sustained through having a sixth part of my farm taken off me for eighteen months practically.

Now these are no fairy tales; the excavation they made in the field is there today, so is the woodland that was felled and hauled, they are there to speak for themselves.

Such is life, and my troubles did not stop here. It was a set job that I had to be hounded off the place and out of the country if it could be done.

I concluded I would quit the land I had taken from Mr. Thomlinson. Although I had got a valueless notice to quit as I was under the Agricultural Land Act I ought to have had twelve months' notice, whereas I only got six months' notice, but I had made up my mind that I would quit peaceably.

So what crop I had standing on the place I commenced to sell. I had no building of any description taken with the land, but, however, the agent had got wind that I was selling the crop, and came down to forbid me selling may *more. I was not at home, but he left a message with my wife that I had to sell no more crops off the place, but I took no heed of his message, and kept selling away; he had no more to do with me than the Kaiser has, and I hope he never will.*

However, the agent's dignity must be adhered to, what he thought right or wrong, and he came down again in a rage and left another message with my wife. He went down to Knot Hill and had a letter sent, forbidding me to sell any more crops off the place.

Well, I thought this behaviour was out of all reason, and it made me think I should be looking after myself and not taking all this nonsense lying down. I thought I had a very good claim for the improvements I had made and the illegal notice I had received to quit the land, so I sent a claim in for £20, and withheld the half year's rent, but, of course, I was on with the upper ten and had no right but to submit quietly.

I received a claim along with the rent owing, making the amount over £50, and a writ was served on me right away. If I had had a choice before, I had none now, so I looked around for a solicitor to defend me. I had never needed one in any of my transactions before, and was advised to engage Mr. Carrick of Brampton. I went and consulted him and he took on my case, stopping the writ, and Mr. Thomlinson entered it for an Assizes Trial.

The mill and land were let by the Earl's stewards. They were up on end and trying to make things as hard as possible for me. They had given me notice to quit Hazel Cottage, the farm I was renting, so I had to prepare to leave this as well; they had let it to a neighbour, so I was sent adrift. I prepared to leave, and at Candlemas I had a sale of stock; what crop I had left was taken at valuation.

The tenant who had taken the farm had Mr. Isaac Rickerby, Aiketgate, and I had Mr. George Armstrong, Ainstable Hill. The referees could find no holes to pick; they were convinced I had all in apple pie order. The crop was all they had to value, and when their valuations were compared there was only £5 difference. We were agreed that the difference should be split, and it was done in less time than I take to write it, so there was no need for any great experts with their college education and their three guineas a day, and up to twelve when they can impose upon their employer, and moreover, make a valuation of £150 and come down to £60 like a lamb, and think they have been clever. My experience is that if they are clever at anything it is over-drinking whisky. These are the sort of men and officials that the Government is stocking the country with.

12

I was busy in the autumn looking for another farm and a home, if one I could find. I had several good, influential friends to speak for me. Mr. James Elliot, Mr. C. Fetherstonhaugh, Staffield Hall, was one that took a deep interest in me; I was born and brought up half a mile off that place. He went over two farms with me, the last one I looked at being Law House. I went to the owner himself but got no encouragement whatever, so I have the job up – give a dog a bad name and you may hang him.

Well, my choice now was to have a house for the wife and wee kiddies, so we took a dander down to Carlisle to take one, and took one off Mr. James Beaty in Myddleton Street. Mr. George Dixon had Petteril Bank land to let, 57 acres in grass, so being a stranger I gave them a bid to pay half year in advance, and I was accepted as tenant, the rent to be £162.10. per annum, £13 odd tythe and over £13 rates, so the rent was stiff for secondary land, but I felt content that I had some work, and a living I would have to try and make.

Candlemas came round and we had a sale and a very nice company, which was encouraging, but I got a letter from the solicitor wanting me to send him a cheque for £60 for action pending. I showed it to the auctioneer, and he, with me, thought he had done nothing for it, but I sent a cheque for the amount to him.

On the 4th of February we set off for a town life, a very rough, snowy morning. The next morning I had a telegram saying my father had passed away, which made us feel very sad in our new abode. He certainly had lived to a ripe old age, eighty-seven years old. I was very pleased that I had

plate 7 - Kirkoswald Church, early 1900s. Thomas's parents are buried in the churchyard. Father William died on 4th February 1879, three years after his mother Ann.

plate 8 - The Red Lion Inn, Armathwaite c.1905

never mentioned my troubles to him so as not to worry him. This was in 1879, thirty-eight years of age.

I began to stock my grassland in March, buying a few Irish cattle at not too big a price. We had a very rough time for snow and frost. I bought two corn-stacks and a hay-stack to give to them, which I never calculated I would want, and two of them died through catching cold. I remember going up on the 6th of May to see them, and there was snow and slush lying on the bottom ground joining Petteril. I went off and took a rough pasture field at Plumpton foot for a month.

It was a fine time the latter end of May, and June weather was all that one could wish for, and having been good to the cattle in cold weather, they went right ahead and grew fat and were no bad job at the finish.

The Assizes came around and I was summoned to attend the court to defend my case. The morning arrived, and my friends drove up to the Red Lion in a wagonette to give evidence, and all was prepared for the eventful day, but before the court opened there was a telegram from Mr. Thomlinson who was in London, saying he was ill. My Council said I could proceed with the case if I chose to, but I said we would not strike lying down. The trial was put off until the following Assizes.

When that day came again we were summoned to appear, and I got all my witnesses gathered up according the Council's instructions, and the court opened with our case first. Mr. Thomlinson was called upon to give evidence, and the judge spoke and said he thought this was a case that should be tried by arbitration, but I told my Council to finish it here. They called another witness, and the judge made the same remark, but I was of a different opinion and told my Council to go on with the case, but he said if we went against the judge's views it might be worse and a hasty decision given, so it was left there and an agent in the court was asked to arbitrate.

There was a judge and jury sitting in that court and a point of law in the case as I had been discharged from the farm with an illegal notice and had witnesses that I had reclaimed the land and made it over anew, but the law is such that a land agent can break any reasonable clause of the kind and upset right or reason; these are the kind of measures they pass and set their seal to in the Houses of Parliament.

Well, the agent's verdict had to be final now, a job that a jury and judge could not decide. I suppose he had to view the place, but he caused an enquiry to be held in the County Hotel, Carlisle. I called my witnesses again, who were Mr. James Elliot of Staffield Hall, Mr. Joseph Dodd, Mr Isaac Ousby, a Lowther farmer, a gentleman often sought to give his opinion, Mr. George Armstrong, Ainstable Hall, and a foreman woodman on the estate. All of them spoke of me making the place over anew, and as for me I had nothing to answer as to the claim. I had no buildings taken with the land, so what could I do but either sell or lead it off the premises. Well, we set two days arbitrating at the County Hotel over a thing a shoe-black could have decided in two hours, if he was not exceptionally dense, but this is not the order of the day, the profession would not get such a pull, and we had to wait a few weeks before the agent gave his award.

This was that I got nothing for being illegally turned off the farm, nothing for making the land over anew, and Mr. Thomlinson was awarded nothing for his claim. But next came the costs. I had given my solicitor three cheques when demanded, one for £60 and two for £50 each, and when he sent his account his claim was for £198.3.0., £160 paid, the balance of £38. I asked him for a bill of particulars, and he never would send me one, so I never gave him the balance; that was how I stood. The agent charged £70 for arbitrating, which was charged to Mr. Thomlinson, and he told a Mr. Kirkbride who went to shoot at his place, that altogether it cost him £700. I could not help but be sorry for Mr. Thomlinson, not forgetting to be sorry for myself. They say, such is life.

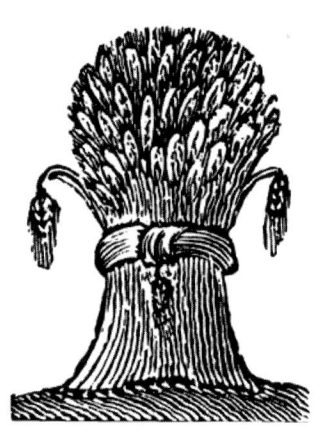

plate 9 - Carlisle Market Place 1897

13

I was at Carlisle now, and with the bit dear land I had taken I was trying to make a living with dealing a bit, and I started to send a few carcasses of mutton to the central meat market, London. My landlord was building a shop and dwelling attached in Myddleton Street, and when it was finished I went into it at Whitsuntide and opened out a retail butcher's shop, taking the business on for 15 months.

I was a good bit away from home, and my wife was harassed, what with the shop and the family, and one Saturday night in July we would put the shutters up so it was no thoroughfare and not a very paying concern, as we closed up. By this time the other storm we had ceased and I had to look farther afield to bring my family up, so I did a bit of cattle and sheep dealing, slaughtering sheep for London and got a living scrambled out.

We shifted into Broad Street, renting a dwelling from Messrs. Irving. I got a few sheep on turnips among the farmers in the winter as well. In November we lost the oldest daughter at the age of ten. She died very suddenly; she was at school on the Monday and died on the Wednesday morning. The doctor said it was the scarlet fever, and that she had got it from some very dirty child and had been poisoned; he had no hope for her from the first. She was a great loss as she was like a mother among the younger children, and was sadly missed, but God ordered it for the best no doubt, and when that time comes, all have to submit to God's will.

Well, I extended by business in the grazing line. I took Durran Hill Park, 50 acres in extent, and one thing to another turned out favourably for me, so I took to extending each line of business I was in. I took Kirklinton Park the year following, 44 acres in extent. Time rolled on and I got to doing a big business in slaughtering sheep for London; I had got into the trade now.

We were in the dwelling five years, and Mr. Beaty was building seven dwelling-houses right opposite where we lived in Broad Street, so I bought three of them and we went to live in one ourselves. I kept the other two a few years, and then sold them over, leaving a small margin of profit. The other one we have yet, having it let.

My inclination was always to farming. The Dean and Chapter had a farm to let where a Mr. Park had been for two years, and he died. This was Newbiggin, Brisco, about 140 acres in extent. I took it over from Mr. Park's executors with the sanction of the Dean and Chapter's agents, on the condition that it had to be revalued at the end of two years. It had been let very dear for the poverty-state it was in.

Mr. Richardson was appointed by the Chapter to value it, and his valuation was £240 per annum. I farmed it ten years, covering 52 acres of it with slaughterhouse dung and blood, laid 37 acres of arable down to grass, took two green crops off it in succession and one of corn, the best and cheapest way of putting land into condition that has been reduced to poverty.

When I gave it up it was let for two years in grass parks. Part I took and part my eldest son took. The dwelling the buildings were tumbling down, or I would not have given it up, we would have lived in it. However, my son took the whole of the land for grazing, with the exception of a small field and meadow. I got comfortably away without any arbitration, paying a claim the Chapter made against me for £6 for some burst drains, so I made no claim for my improvements. My son is farming the land yet.

plate 10 – The Market Place, Carlisle c.1900

14

In 1895 my family was growing up and leaving school, five sons and two daughters, and their inclination was all bent on farming. My second son was serving his time to be a grocer, and although he served his full time, he also was bent on farming.

Lowthian Gill came into the market to be let, so I have a bid for it as I thought Carlisle streets were no place to turn the family on to learn farming. The Mrs of the house had brought them up not to parade the streets; they had to prepare for bed at six o'clock every night until after they had left school.

Farming had been no great game for a few years at that time, and no likelihood of times mending. It was a big undertaking, but I bid the agents £400 a year for it for the two first years and £500 for the remainder, for a lease of twenty-one years, with a break at the end of fourteen years. I thought that in taking the place on a long lease I could set to and improve the land and place, and started off at the very first to do that. I bought the majority of the crops at the farm sale, and seven stacks of corn at the sale of a farm adjoining mine. Had a week's threshing; the corn brought me 5/6d per bushel, with the straw left for the labour. Certainly corn was at a low ebb then, worth from 6/6d to 7/3d per bushel, and the price never rose during the fourteen years I was on the farm.

It was entirely a tillage farm and had been hungered. I took the farm on to improve it, or I knew we could not live on it, so I commenced to break the land out of lea in the autumn for turnips without taking a white crop off first. I took a white crop after a green crop, and I still got a good crop that way, which was better than two light crops doing it in the ordinary way, at the same time getting the land into heart; there is no cheaper or better way of bringing land around that has been impoverished.

My landlord was an old gentleman living in Manchester. He did the agency for a time himself, and was doing his duty by putting the place in order. I never had the pleasure of seeing him, all our business being done by letter, and as far as my experience went he was a gentleman with tact and judgment. It only lasted for about eighteen months or two years, when I suppose he became poorly and not considered fit to do his own business, and an enquiry was made as to the state of his mind.

plate 11 – Lowthian Gill farmhouse

He was a gentleman who had never married, and his heirs were a brother and sisters and their families. When the enquiry was made one of his nephews came to Lowthian Gill and asked for the correspondence that I had had with my landlord. I was not at home, but my wife gave him the letters that I had received, on the conditions that he returned them, but that he forgot to do. Perhaps it did not matter much to me, and it was left there.

After the enquiry an agent was appointed by the heirs to look over his estates, and as far as my judgment went he was the most competent gentleman in that line of business that ever I met, and he was doing everything up to date that needed repairs, the gutters and drains excepted, but of course I thought he would attend to them through time. It was specially mentioned in the lease that the landlord had to keep the drains in repair.

When I entered the farm a gentleman from Carlisle had the game and shooting taken, and he had still two years to go. After the two years expired he gave it up, so my eldest son and a Mr. Dawson professed to a bit of sport, so I took the shooting from the agent for £10 per annum and let the two have the job and they gave it up, so I relet it to a Carlisle gentleman, along with the rabbits, for £30. The gentleman had it for a year, and then another firm from Carlisle took it for the same rent.

It was getting on to the shooting season, and the agent landed at the door one day and I thought there was something displeasing him. I asked him into the house, and as soon as he took a seat he broke off and said a nephew of the landlord and a friend wanted a day's shooting over the place. I told him I had the shooting let, and he said I should not have let it. However, I had done so and he was angry about it. I was sorry as we did not part such good friends as usual.

A little while after that I had a letter from him that I had to repair a wall adjoining some rough ground I had on condition I paid the rates, and it proved very dear at that. It had been a plantation with no eatage on it to do good for stock, in fact eventually it did harm as the herbage was so poor they could not digest it.
At all events when the late tenant went over the land with a land agent and myself, he pointed out that the landlord repaired, so it was understood that the tenant had nothing to do with it. I wrote him to that effect, and also about some more repairs they had to do and which had not been attended to, and also the drains which had to be put right by the landlord, and which had not been touched.

However, the agent came with a joiner and they did all the repairs in a creditable way, with the exception of the draining, and he set a drainer to work a while after, opening drains out. He was there for a week and made no better of them. They had been put in so deep that the sides rushed in as he took the soil out, and he gave it up and left it. There were three fields badly affected in this way, to the extent of 80 acres, and 56 acres of it I could not till on account of the broken drains, and the highway road matter that was allowed to run over them, through the neglect of the Rural District Council.

Well, I got notice to quit the shooting just before another shooting season came on. A Mr. Scott, a nephew of my landlord's, came to the place and told me that he and Mr. Edwards of Armathwaite Castle had taken the shooting, and they were going to put a game-keeper on the place and were going to bring a foreign sort of partridge into an 8 acre plantation, and they wanted me to make sure that nothing disturbed them.

Mr. Scott seemed to me a thorough gentleman, and I said I would do my best, but I never saw Mr. Scott anymore. Mr. Edwards and a Mr. Sandyman did the shooting over the place, and we got on very well while I was there. They were very kind to me, and thorough gentlemen in every respect.

Well, the estate was put into the hands of a fresh steward to look after and receive the rents. I approached him about the burst drains, but the only answer I got was that the landlord would drain if I led the tiles and paid interest for the money expended. I told him that was not in concord with my agreement, but there was nothing done to them, which caused a very great sacrifice to me.

I heard that the gamekeeper engaged to look after the land had arrived. My men saw him occasionally, likewise a son who went to the Manchester Market. He had seen him once at Armathwaite station and another time on the road, and said he was drunk both times.

I happened to be down paying rent to the agent at Carlisle, and he asked me how the gamekeeper was getting on. I told him that I had never seen him, but that my son has seen him twice and that he was drunk both times. The agent said point-blank that he did not believe it. "Well", I says, "I can believe it".

There was some three years before the fourteen years of my lease expired. Time rolled on and I gave my landlord notice that I was going to quit the place at the end of fourteen years. The agents advertised the farm to let, and appointed a neighbour to show over the farm, saying nothing to me about it. However, I met one of the firm's land agents, and told him I did not mind taking it on if they would do the repairs and draining free of cost to me.

They sent word to that effect to the landlord, and he appointed a day when he would meet me at the land agent's office. No doubt he was a proper gentleman and proposed spending £360 on the place free of interest, but I stuck out for paying no interest on any money he invested in repairs, etc. I expected my son meeting me there and told them so, and said I would go and bring him in; he was the only son left with me at the time, the other four sons and a daughter were married, and on their own. I met him and we went back to the office, but my son thought I should not budge from my offer, so we did not come to any arrangement.

However, the land agent followed us out and asked us to go back as the landlord wanted me to take the place on, but my son said we would have nothing more to do with it, and I was not surprised as he and all the family had worked like niggers, the times being at their worst for farming, and if it had not been for the help I got from my family I would have been getting the Old Age Pension today, or it might have been the Workhouse.

15

The time drew near for us leaving the place, and I had a joiner in to repair all doors, gates and fences, so that no one could come after me and claim for them; the land also was thoroughly clear of any dirt. A Mr. Young had taken the place. Two auctioneers approached me about the farm sale, but I thought I would try and be my own auctioneer. I approached Mr. Young and offered him a lot of the implements, carts and gear and the remainder I sold to neighbouring farmers and dealers. At the finish I just had the horses left, and these I sold at Hetherington's Auction Mart on Candlemas Term Saturday. When all was settled I calculated that I was not less than £200 into pocket through doing my own business instead of holding a Candlemas sale.

We were due to leave Lowthian Gill on February 22nd, 1909. when I bought Micklethwaite Farm for my son and daughter, I also bought another farm at Ghyll Head, Rosley for myself, and as my son, daughter, wife and myself had all agreed to live under one roof, and that I was to be the farmer, the question arose as to which of the farms we should live at. I selected Micklethwaite, where we are today.

Now the formalities invented by our great statesmen in farming the Agricultural Holdings Act, in conjunction with the agreement made between the landlord and myself, had to be gone through. They make laws in the House of Commons and the unworthy can grab at things they shouldn't be allowed to.
Well, I went to the agent and offered to settle the business between the landlord and myself as to claims under the Act

and my agreement, but he said no, it would have to go through the usual formalities. Of course, I made a claim for unexhaustive improvements and cake consumed on the farm, and thought I was entitled to a substantial sum under the present conditions of things.

During the fourteen years I had farmed the place £7,000 (seven thousand pounds) worth of cake had been consumed, apart from the corn of my own growing, I had used bran and other meals, together with several stacks I had bought at farm sales. During the last three years of my tenancy I had paid £1,600 for cake alone, and the only crop I ever sold off the place was one solitary small stack of hay, that a neighbour who was short of hay asked me to sell to him. I asked the agent's permission to sell it and this was given in a grudging manner. I did not get a straight answer that I could do so at the time, but permission came after a bit.

I had farmed the land in order to improve it just as if I was the proprietor, only taking one white crop and one green crop off it in rotation, and at that, most of it was done in a seven years' course.

I got a land agent to make out my claim and he put it at £490, but at the time I thought this was a good deal more than I was entitled to, so I asked another friend of mine, who was an expert on feeding stuffs, etc., and he made it out accurately that I was entitled to a little over £180 to keep under my due.

The agents who had the business to conduct in connection with the farm sent a claim in against me, but I could not surmise what it was for. The landlord's agents chose three others to act as umpires, and gave me the option to choose one of them to act for me. Well the agent I had employed

"CROFTON HALL."

3,703 Acres.   Rents, £4,502 8 0.

TO BE SOLD BY AUCTION.

In the County Estate Auction Rooms, The Crescent, Carlisle,
on Wednesday, May 20th, 1908,
AT 2 O'CLOCK IN THE AFTERNOON PROMPT.

In One or more Lots, unless previously Sold by Private Treaty.

fig. 3 – Sale details from the Crofton Hall estate catalogue 1908

MICKLETHWAITE FARM.

Two Dwelling Houses and Ranges of Suitable Farm Buildings, together with a Cottage and 262 Acres 2 Roods 2 Poles of Arable, Meadow, and Pasture Land, in the Occupation of Mr. Archibald Ritson as Yearly Tenant.

SCHEDULE.

Ordnance No.	Description	Acreage.
192 Part.	House, Buildings and Stackyard (West)	1·224
200	House, Buildings and Yard (East)	·345
201	Cottage and Garden	·557
191 Part.	Orchard	·230
196	Paddock	·515
199	,,	·327
716	Meadow	9·255
189	Pasture	13·606
198	Meadow	1·680
714	,,	·285
202	,,	2·292
713	,,	·316
203	Pasture	·916
204	,,	7·707
205	,,	3·261
157	Arable	15·345
158	Meadow	14·380
159	Arable	10·826
160	Pasture	8·342
194	,,	6·048
172	Meadow	1·991
170	Pasture	2·305
84	,,	2·374
85	Arable	5·173
169	,,	8·773
168	,,	10·103
87	,,	9·830

Ordnance No.	Description	Acreage
162	Arable	4·080
163	,,	5·019
92	,,	10·224
93	,,	6·028
94	,,	7·314
96	,,	8·227
98	,,	10·147
99	,,	7·400
101	,,	13·305
79	,,	7·070
176	,,	7·078
76	Meadow	3·120
75	,,	8·953
727	,,	·203
725	,,	1·172
180	Pasture	3·740
181	,,	6·276
182	Meadow	5·936
32 Part.	Parton Mire	7·220
65 Part.	,,	2·000
		262·518

MICKLETHWAITE FARM—*Continued.*

The Apportioned Rent of this Farm is £383 1s. 4d.

Plan of Micklethwaite farm, Wigton c.1900

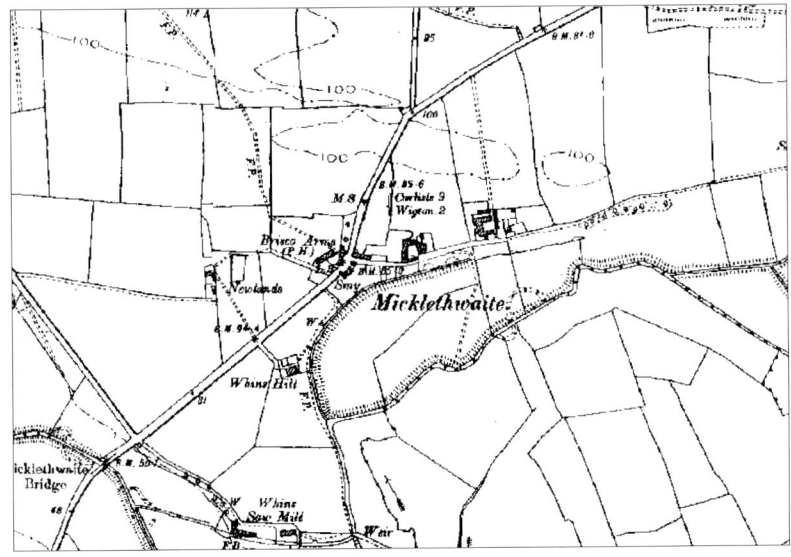

GILLHEAD FARM.

Coloured Pink on the accompanying Plan.

A DWELLING HOUSE AND EXTENSIVE RANGE OF SUITABLE FARM BUILDINGS, TOGETHER WITH 146 ACRES 2 ROODS 23 POLES OF ARABLE, MEADOW, AND PASTURE LAND, IN THE OCCUPATION OF MR. WILLIAM ARMSTRONG AS ANNUAL TENANT.

SCHEDULE.

Ordnance No.	Description	Acreage
1788	House, Buildings, Cottage, &c.	2·091
1787	Wood	·519
1784	Arable	12·270
1783	,,	11·294
1775	,,	11·566
1694	Road	·189
1902	,,	·875
1774	Arable	13·472
1903	,,	10·777
1899	,,	14·722
1898	,,	13·516
1789	Pasture	17·298
1790	Arable	5·616
1795	,,	5·072
1796	,,	5·645
1776	,,	21·722
		146·644

The Apportioned Annual Rent of this Lot is £177 6 5
Cottage 9 0 0
£186 6 5

fig. 4

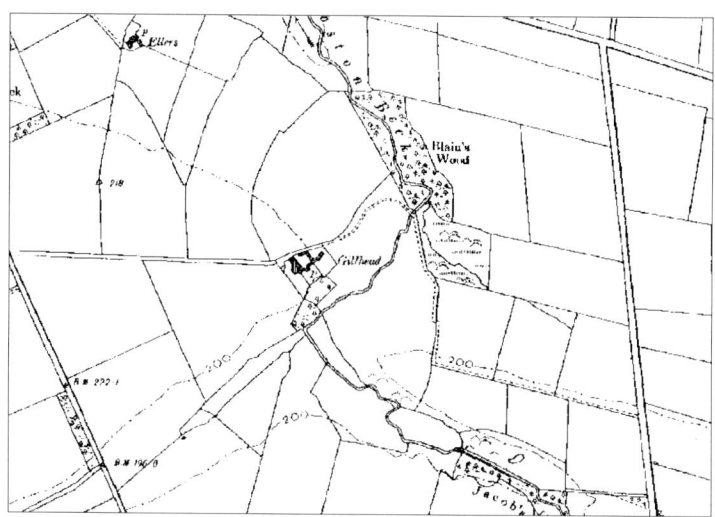

Plan of Gill Head farm, Rosley c.1900

preferred a man from Carlisle; he was not my choice at all, but of course I gave in as the agent had been employed by me to arbitrate.

The day appointed was late in March or the first week in April, a good while after I had left, but they are busy men, land agents, with their three guineas a day, and some of them three times that amount.

There had been two fox hunts and a great ploughing day on the place between the time of my leaving and this date, and the parties were viewing the place as they had caused a few breaks in the fences. However, they started to go round the land and the fences. The landlord's agent, another forward sort of youth and the umpire began shaking the fences. I thought no one but the umpire had any right to do that, so I called their attention to it, and the novice was called off. It was splendid day, and the umpire was furnished with a basket of sandwiches and rum, whisky, brandy and bottled ale; he might have had champagne as well; Mr. and Mrs. Young, the hostess of the house, were exceedingly kind, and we had tea in the house; it was like a Sunday out.

They did not finish that day, it was too good a job for them to get through it in a hurry, and as for myself I could not see that there was anything they could find fault with. The landlord's agent drew the umpire's attention to a field in stubble as he thought it should not be so, but it was the same when I entered on, and I had only taken two crops of corn off it in fourteen years. There was another field called Ivy Cottage field, half of which was oats and half grass. This was not right for them, but how they came to make that out they never explained. It had been an extra heavy crop of oats, and it had a good right to be as I had covered it with slaughterhouse dung which I had carted six miles from Carlisle. There was a field of 28 acres lying up on the heights of Barrock, and they complained it was not a very good set of seeds. I had been told by the two previous tenants' sons that it had never had any seeds on it worth calling seeds, and that they took their oaths to swear.

Well, the great men got the work finished, and the enquiry was to be held at Carlisle, but they could not fix the time as one was going to one place and another to some other place on certain days. Well, I thought, it was a general harvest among land agents, and as for myself, I was never consulted as to which day would suit me.

However, I received notice sometime after that they were going to hold the enquiry on a certain day, and I was told that the landlord's agents were engaging a solicitor, so of course I thought we should be up-to-date and employed one to conduct my case.

They had engaged the very gentleman I took the farm off, and I was pleased as I knew he would know the state of the place when I got it.

Well, my witnesses were called first and they testified as to how I had improved the land. I had 180 acres of grain the last harvest I was there, and I threshed 100 acres of it out of stook and consumed the whole of the 100 acres of straw that it grew and three stacks we threshed out in the winter besides. They complained of there being too little dung left, although I had used two-thirds of what I grew. The oncoming farmer had led the dung out and spread it on the land, so they could not tell, but, of course, they must have something to say.

Now when I went to the place I erected a wooden byre to hold twelve cattle and another building that was of little use I made into a byre to hold twelve more cattle, and all at my own expense, and I certainly had them all full during the winters I was there. I also put up a good sheep-dipping place, and cemented out another house in which to slaughter, but none of these was set at anything by the umpire, so I had to give in to the inevitable.

The landlord's agent had been making ready for eventualities. Sixteen months before he had taken a man on to my farm to see if they could find out anything that was not up-to-date, and likely all they could find fault with was a 28 acre field on the heights of Barrock. This man brought forward the fact that he had made an inspection of the same at the end of October, and he made it out that it was not clear of faults; it had been eaten off with sheep and there was nothing growing on it.

When I entered on the farm this same field was over-run with dirt. It had been sown with turnips, and on the ploughing day the men could not keep their ploughs in the ground for dirt choking them, and how I managed to get rid of this was a marvel to myself. I attributed it to ploughing it deep out of lea in the autumn and harrowing it and allowing it to lie all winter. Most of the dirt rotted away, and by turniping the field and working it late on it killed the other.

The arbitrator and umpire put great stress on the seeds not being good, but Mr. Bulman, son of a former farmer who had been on it for seventeen years, and also the son of the last tenant, both declared they never saw seeds on the same field worth anything. It was clover sick, and because it was on a high latitude away from the farmhouse it had got neither farm dung nor lime carted to it; it had always been managed with artificial manure. Where they got the damage they put on for dilapidations I was at a loss to know, also my witnesses.

There used to be gibbet on Barrock where people were hanged for their misdemeanours, but, of course, things are looked in a more humane way these days.
During the court day we stopped a short time for luncheon, and my solicitor told me that the way the umpire was hanging to the other side we had a poor chance, so when the case was wound up the expected happened. My solicitor and arbitrator both made a very moderate charge, and my witnesses would have nothing for their day. They were Mr. Wallace, Hayclose, Mr. Bullman, Wragmire, Mr. Walton, Boustead Hill, Mr. Thomlinson, Cumwhinton, Mr. Beatty, Barrockside, and the joiner who put the place in repair. "Well", thinks I to myself, "this is a rosy job, when an umpire has the power to give a decision as he likes and feather his cap out of hardworking farmers".

16

Well, we got to Micklethwaite in 1909, on to a farm that my son and daughter bought, or at least I bought it for them, acting as agent, and I farmed it myself up to Candlemas 1917 and now my son and daughter are farming it on their own account.

When we entered on, the farmer had two farms, both about the same area, and when we entered he removed to the other place which was not sold. He led the principal part of the manure on to the place where he was going to reside, led and sold all the crop off it, and had wasted most of the good thorn fences through neglect and bad management. There were 250 yards of one fence which had been repaired by taking a cartload of thorns and putting them in with a pitchfork until it was about 2 yards broad; mind this was a boundary fence, and thorns covering the gutters.

The farmer's son went round with us to show the fences and boundary and he said there never was any gutter, but we pulled thorns and rubbish out, railed it and set it with thorns and there is a gutter now.

Other things had been neglected, but I thought at the time I had had enough of land agents so I took the thing lying down and ate humble pie, although I was advised on good authority that the farmer could be made to pay for the dung he had led off the place and for putting the fences and other things into repair, but who would reap the benefit but the land agents who neither sow nor reap. I began to make improvements to the place. The tenant who was leaving told me that I would see the holmes all covered with water some morning when I got up, which I suppose had happened when there was a flood.

I had been told that watered grass was no good to stock very early in life, so I engaged a man to put a foot on the embankment for about 250 to 300 yards and stop up all the rat and mole holes. This embankment was to keep the River Wampool in its course, and there has been no flood on that land for eight years.

There were about 25 acres of that land which were subject to flooding, so I basic slagged and lime composted the whole, and put cake and feeding stuff on for cattle and sheep, and the land speaks for itself, I put about 1,000 yards of lime and compost on to the remainder of the meadow and pasture land, as well as covering it with farmyard manure; drained some wet meadow-land which had been flooded purposely to make it grow grass, repaired the buildings and spouted the whole of them, and did as much as I could.

Candlemas 1917, I gave up the place to my son and daughter so that they could farm it themselves, and this year the Committee gave them notice that they had to plough 35 acres of corn for 1918 crop. This cruel war upsets everything. The population must be fed, but whether the authorities are taking a right view of things, enforcing land which has been managed on the face to any extra extent, and omitting land which had lain for a generation and giving it nothing extra to make it grow, and as it is, carrying a sheep to the acre. This land had all been ploughed and corned formerly, and ploughing it now would improve it and turning it up afresh it would grow a good crop.

This is a question which needs to be worked out by thoroughly competent and practical men, and not pounced upon by a lot of paid agents who know very little about it. I am certain this wants due consideration. Of course the population has to be fed, but if you can get as much crop off the land that is worth very little as it is, as you can get off land that is worth £5 to £10 per acre lying as it is in grass or growing hay for two or three years, it is worth a trial. There is possibly another way of looking at it; the good land might very possibly grow a crop that would lodge and be a middling harvest, it would be worth very little, whereas the bad land would be worth equally as much for corn when turned up afresh for three or four or five years. The land that has been managed on the face and lying low and sheltered from bad weather would be worth ten times as much for rearing and feeding stock. This question wants due consideration, and not gone into, this great necessity, blindfolded.

plate 12 - Gill Head farmhouse

17

During a number of years when we were at Carlisle and Lowthian Gill I did a fairly large business in turniping sheep on farms. It was a great business at one time, taking turnips by the week for shearlings and aged wethers which were bought all over the West and North of Scotland, but the business is practically finished now, for two reasons. It is young light mutton that is wanted, and farmers are breeding and buying them themselves to feed. A very good idea when they are both their own horn and their own corn; they can make considerably more mutton to feed the population, and that is a great advantage to the consumer as well as to the feeder.

When I speak of feeding sheep, I have bought sheep from the greatest part of Scotland in fairly large numbers, including most of the Isles. I have considerable dealings in the Isle of Skye, Isle of Mull, Isle of Jura.

I can say this, I had to borrow a good deal of capital when I was doing any extensive business that way, and I was never refused any money I wanted with the exception of once at the bank, and I moved my quarters right away, though I did not exactly blame the manager. I had a kind friend who spoke a good word for me, and I had traded with the same bank for fifteen years, and they wanted me to go back, but one bitten, twice shy, and I have done business with the London City and Midland Bank ever since, for over thirty years.

I sometimes joined an old acquaintance in the turniping transaction. Mr. Sam Blackley of March Hill, Dumfries, and I had 1,600 sheep from Skye. This was my first partnership business and we brought the whole lot into Cumberland, turniped them among the farmers, and had the whole of the marketing myself. Mr. Blackley has been gone many years, but his son John is carrying the business on still, and I have had many transactions with him since.

Mr. Joseph Thompson, late of Kirkoswald, was another schoolmate and long friend with whom I was in company in turniping sheep pretty extensively. He has gone to his long home, and when I look round I do not see many in the trade who started life with me; they have gone to their long rest, and my turn cannot be long when I will have to follow. I would not have done this scribbling but for an object I have in view, and I hope it will be prosperous for the cause for which I aim it.

plate 13 – Sheep clipping at Swarthbeck Farm, Pooley Bridge c.1910

Now turniping sheep was not a sociable business at all times. The turnips were bought by the consumer by week for sheep; the sheep were sent to the farmer who had his capital invested in them, and he wanted them to grow fat and pay. The farmer owned the turnips, and of course he wanted to make the most he could out of the turnips; he had his rent to pay and an expensive crop to grow. So the turnips are given to the sheep in breaks to last a fortnight or ten days; the first eight days they have a good time on it, and the last two days that are cleaning a break up, and often are not getting what they should and losing what they have gained. Sometimes it happens that the farmer is busy the day the sheep should be moved, busy threshing or going to market, and the sheep are hungered and when they get a fresh break of turnips, two or three of them will eat too many and die. The sheep could be made better in ten weeks than some farmers would make them in twenty, and if this happened scores of times the farmer would frown if spoken to, and would make out he a gentleman himself even if he was hungering your sheep.

18

There is but one really honest, straight course to take to reap the full benefit out of the soil for the good of the nation at large. It is very simple, and is this. Let the owner of the land let it to the best advantage to himself, but the people say it must be put to the best possible use to the nation that mankind can devise.

As the Scriptures say, the road is wide that leadeth to destruction, but narrow is the road that leadeth to life everlasting. And so it is today with the staple that the existence of the nation depends on. What is the remedy? We have been living in a fool's paradise, getting our food at a cheap rate and neglecting a staple of vital importance at home. We cannot recall the past, but the use of the land needs to be cultivated in the very best interests of the nation. How is that to be honestly done? There is no need to kick a landowner because he has got it honestly enough, if he has inherited it or bought it, it will belong the rightful owner the same as any other personal or private property belongs to the rightful owner, or a man that has worked honestly for his day's wage. It would be considered very wicked if they had to be kicked because they had done what was just and right to get hold of such. What more the owner of the land?

When we look over the landscape and the dwelling houses and buildings erected by our forefathers, and which have been allowed to crumble for want of repair, and no new ones erected in their places. Is it not a disgrace for a prosperous nation otherwise to look at? When we look at the landscape and see the well-set out fields and hedges, how they have been cast and planted with thorn, and the land guttered and drained, and ponds and lakes that were injurious to crops and vegetation taken away, and look at the same now. The tiller of the soil in most instances has not the grace or spirit in him to repair them, although he signs a scrap of paper that he will do so. Is it not a shame that it should be so?

The majority of farmers run away and leave the urgent business at home in order to go to markets and auction marts three or four days in the week, whether on business or not, and their own establishments are neglected. If the different tradesmen in the town were to run away and leave their businesses to the wind in the same manner, their places would not be as neat as they are, nor yet would their profits.

The farmers go to the auction marts to help them to pay their big dividends and their officials a big salary. No wonder they can build castles in which to sell stock when they had a countryside of farmers and dealers working two days in the week for them for nothing. There never was any need for auction marts, and there is still less now when stick is sold by weight. Could not all these highly-paid auctioneers, managers, clerks and other officials be found a more important job in the national interest?

There is a terrible outcry about profiteering among different parts of the community and gentlemen responsible for the welfare of the state. Does this never occur to them in connection with the present system of purveying stock? Instead of being sold to go to the pastures on which they will be fed, they are knocked about from auction to auction for a week or fortnight before they find a home, and they are huddled up together in an auction mark for eight or ten hours.

I have seen stock being sold at 9 o'clock at night in an auction, and perhaps the same stock left home at 5 o'clock in the morning, and then have to stand in the pens until the next morning before they could be moved.

The question is; what abuse is the stock getting, and how will the animals deteriorate with such treatment? Is this not a national as well as an individual loss? And what about the company of farmers and dealers watching them going through this process, when they could be better employed at home or elsewhere? No one need be puzzled at auctioneers and their officials walking about all week, treating their friends, when they have a countryside working for them for nothing.

If these men were at home looking after the business they have there it would be more profitable for them. If they reckon themselves at 5/- a day less than they pay a man for the day, they would benefit themselves instead of wasting their time and paying people for doing business which they ought to be capable of doing themselves.

A dealer who is buying eight or ten wagons of sheep privately off a farmer at home, and sending them right away to a provincial market where they are needed, is doing more good to the country than a roadful of auctioneers and their officials.

If the farmers are not fit to sell their own stock, they are scarcely fit to own it. If they do not think themselves capable, they should let their wives or daughters sell the *stock. They do their own business in selling their butter, eggs, poultry, and yet the man has to look on like a dummy until someone else does his business for him. It is no wonder the women want the franchise, and moreover, they deserve it.*

plate 14 - Thomas and Mary Anne's headstone at Ainstable churchyard.
Thomas died October 18th 1919, aged 77 years old
Mary Anne died March 17th 1918, aged 74 years old
baby William, daughter Grace and son John Salkeld
are also named on the headstone.

Plate 15 – St.Michael & All Angels Church, Ainstable   c.1950

Ainstable church witnessed numerous Irving family events during the 19th century including christenings, marriages and burials.
William married Ann Lowther on October 25th 1824
Thomas married Mary Anne Rain on September 10th 1870.

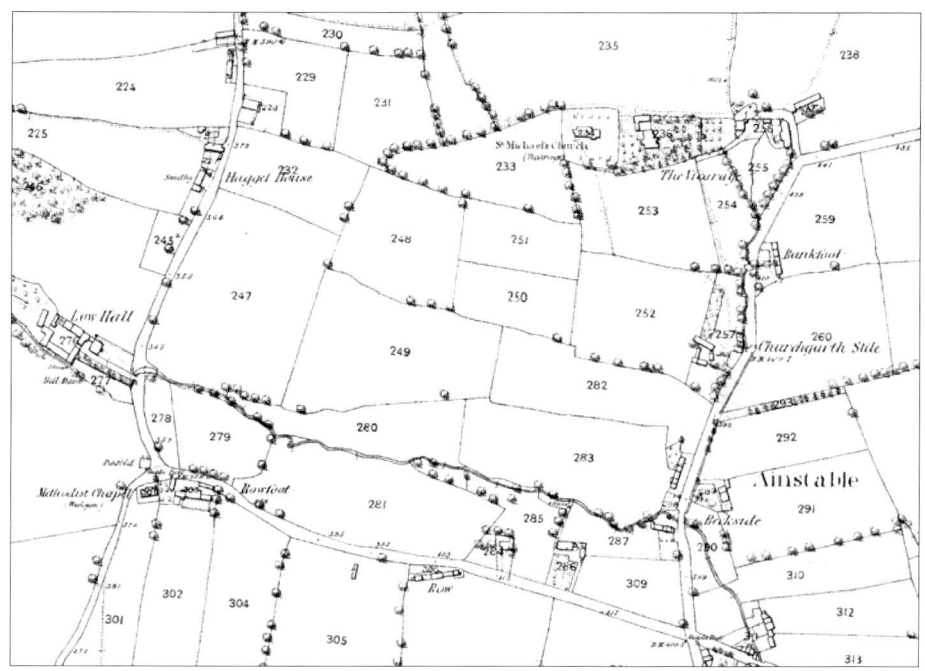

Map of Ainstable 1895

If you think you are a descendant of Thomas Irving the publishers would like to hear from you. Please write to Wagtail Press, Gairshield, Whitley Chapel, Hexham, Northumberland NE47 0HS or email: wagtailpress@yahoo.co.uk.

Please look at our range of local history books:
www.wagtailpress.co.uk

Index of Farms & Places mentioned by Thomas Irving

(In addition to his frequent references to Penrith & Carlisle)

Aiketgate 58
Ainstable 37, 39, 58, 60, 93, 94, 95
Alston 34, 44, 45
Armathwaite 47, 49- 52, 54, 71
Bampton 29
Barnard Castle 34
Barrockside 82
Bellingham 24, 25
Bewcley 23
Blunderfield 9, 17, 18, 39, 43
Boustead Hill 82
Brampton 57
Broadfield 27
Broomhall 22
Broughill fair 29
Burnt House 26, 47
Castle Carrock 19
Clifton 28
College Park 45
Corbridge 26
Craglin 19
Crindledyke 10
Crookdyke Mill 27
Cumwhinton 82
Durdar House Farm 35
Durran Hill Park 65
Eumont Bridge 21, 22
Fosterly (Frosterly) 34
Garsdale 35, 37
Ghyll Head (Gill Head) 78, 85
Great Salkeld 18, 19
Hayclose 82
Hazel Cottage Farm 49, 51, 57

Hexham 23
High Wool Oaks 33
Highbank Hill 35, 45
Kempley Brow 22
Kirkby Stephen 34, 35
Kirklinton Park 66
Kirkoswald 19, 37, 87
Knot Hill 57
Langwathby 23
Little Dockray 21
Little Salkeld 35
Low Grounds 44
Lowthian Gill 68, 70, 74, 86
Maidenhill 27
Micklethwaite 74, 76, 77, 83
Newbiggin 17, 18, 26, 66
Newcastle Water Works 24
Ousby 20
Petteril Bank 59, 61
Plumpton 30, 35, 37, 61
Ricerton (Riccarton) railway 25
Rock Lodge 54
Roman Way 35
Sedburgh 37
Southwaite 23
Springfield 35, 45
Staffield 39, 43, 59
Talkin Fell 19
Thornthwaite Hall 27, 28, 29, 30
Wallmersyke Mill 19
Walmersyke 45
Wath 19
Westgarth Hill 10
Wragmire 82